A YEAR IN PSYCHOLOGY

CONNOR WHITELEY

No part of this book may be reproduced in any form or by any electronic or mechanical means. Including information storage, and retrieval systems, without written permission from the author except for the use of brief quotations in a book review.

This book is NOT legal, professional, medical, financial or any type of official advice.

Any questions about the book, rights licensing, or to contact the author, please email connorwhiteley@connorwhiteley.net

Copyright © 2023 CONNOR WHITELEY

All rights reserved.

DEDICATION

Thank you to all my readers without you I couldn't do what I love.

INTRODUCTION

When I was looking for a psychology placement as part of my degree, I wished there was a book or something for me to read from a real placement student so I could understand what it was like.

Because let's face it, whenever we hear placement students talking about their experiences we know that there are people from the university close by. Meaning the placement students are probably never ever going to say anything bad about their placements.

But they can't be all perfect.

Therefore, as an author of over 20 psychology books and even more fiction books, I decided to write my own so I could tell placement students about my own experiences.

Since in the 2021/2022 academic year, I am doing a psychology research placement where I am conducting research with a Senior lecturer at my university and one of his PhD students.

Also I promise you this book is filled with more general tips and pieces of information on placements as a whole. Therefore, even if you aren't doing an academic placement then you will still find this book useful.

Who Is This Book For?

Whether you're looking for a placement or on a placement, you will still find this interesting book useful. As you will hear my honest experiences about different aspects of the placement through a series of reflections.

Together we'll cover a lot of different aspects to placements so you can understand what it is like in my experience. As well as if you are on a placement then you can know you aren't alone in what you're experiencing, or learning.

Who Am I?

I fully admit this is a very different sort of book compared to my normal fact-based, engaging and fascinating psychology books. But I still always like to know who writes the nonfiction books I read, so I know the information is reliable.

In case you're like me, I am a psychology student from the University of Kent, England and I am the host of the weekly The Psychology World Podcast available on all major podcast apps and YouTube.

Also I am the author of a lot of psychology books, including my bestselling Forensic Psychology and Criminal Profiling.

But most importantly, I am doing a placement year as part of my psychology degree.

In the rest of the book, you'll explore what is a placement, why you might want to do one and then we'll explore what is my experience and what you can learn from it.

So now the introduction is done, let's explore the amazing world of psychology placements!

WHAT IS A PSYCHOLOGY PLACEMENT AND WHAT ARE THE BENEFITS?

I know that universities never explain what a placement is very well, so I want to explain it now.

A placement/ placement year is a year of work experience between your second and third year of university where you work in a certain setting or place for at least 30 weeks and it always has something to do with your degree.

For instance, some examples of a psychology placement would be:

- Working In A Mental Health Service, like the UK's NHS.
- Doing psychology research at a university.
- Working in a Human Resource department (for business psychology students).

There are plenty more settings and environments

that you can work in as part of your placement.

But you all need to remember is a psychology placement, is a year (or 30 weeks) of psychology work experience.

Which is brilliant for the reasons I'll mention in a moment, but I want to add that there will be some coursework as part of your placement.

In my experience, there are two main pieces of coursework, a series of reflections that get you to reflect on what you've learnt, what you want to learn and how your placement is helping your personal and professional development.

This is why this book is a series of reflections because it is an expanded version of my coursework, but of course the really honest reflections, I will not be sending to the university. That's for you.

Then the other part of your coursework will be some sort of research report that you have to write.

Now I know a lot of students (including me at first) hated this, but this is actually great and it gives us a massive advantage over other students. For the sole reason that when we go into our final year we would have had an extra year of practicing how to conduct and write research to a high level.

Meaning our dissertation should be easier because we could have extra experience on researching and writing up a professional report.

As well as another great thing about placement coursework is that it's pass or fail, meaning there is no harsh grade that could influence your final degree marks.

In addition, you might have to do a poster presentation on your placement that explains what it was like, what you learnt and more. That is a piece of my coursework but because I'm not at the stage yet I'm not including it here as a major piece of coursework.

Of course, depending on your university, you might have other pieces of coursework or there might be slight variations in what I have explained, but as with everything in this book, this is my experience as a placement student.

What Are The Benefits of Doing A Placement?

In case you bought this book to investigate placement years as an option or you know you want to do one, but you want to learn more. For the rest of the chapter, I'm going to be explaining the great benefits of placement opportunities.

So this is where I can be very honest because the massive problem with university is they teach you all the theory and a LOT of practical things with essays, assignments and exams (that you never do in the real-world).

But!

But they never ever give you real world experience and that is the downfall of many degrees.

For example, when I choose to go to university, I knew I was only going to do a "real" degree and by that I mean I was only going to do a degree that had a job at the end of it.

Meaning there was a job that only I could get because I had a degree in the subject.

This is why I choose psychology because you cannot get a job in psychology without a degree. And the exact same goes for subjects like medicine, Law, all the sciences and more.

However, even though I choose a degree that means I wouldn't have to "fight" off non-graduates for a job. All psychology students will have to compete with each other the jobs and postgraduate opportunities.

As after you get your degree, you are about one in thousands with the exact same degree.

So what could help you make yourself more attractive to these employers and universities?

Experience.

Everyone wants experience these days and that is the massive benefit you can get from a placement. Since placements will allow you to work in the real world, develop new skills and learn things that the classroom doesn't teach you.

Because since I started my placement, I've learnt more about certain modern topics that the psychology classroom won't teach you and my academic writing has improved drastically.

Which as we all know, university just presumes you can write academically.

Additionally, another great benefit of placements is you can use them as testers. As you can go on placement to somewhere and test out how you feel about the setting and if you can see yourself working there in the future.

For example, you might think you love working in a child mental health setting as part of your clinical psychology degree. But when it comes to your placement and you work there, you realise you hate it and you vow never to work in this setting again.

That's great.

As you used your placement to find out what you liked and didn't like so you can avoid making the same mistake with your "real-world" job in the future. And as we can guess and probably know, it's a lot harder to suddenly change your mind and change jobs in the real-world.

So it's best to make a "mistake" in your choosing of jobs now than in the future when you could potentially be stuck with your chosen setting for longer than you want.

Overall, I do actively encourage everyone to do a placement degree if they can because it can give you amazing work experience that will help you with the job market after university.

Of course, having a placement and work experience doesn't guarantee anything, but it can help. And we all need that.

But why did I choose a placement?

WHY DID I CHOOSE A PSYCHOLOGY PLACEMENT?

Building upon what I mentioned in the last chapter, I want to talk about my own reasons for choosing a placement so you can understand why I'm doing this, and some of my reasons might resonate with you.

Therefore, back in 2018/2019 when I started to look at different psychology degrees for me. I noticed two universities offered these very different degrees and they were degrees with placement years.

Making me immediately hooked on those degrees because I wanted to do that mainly for the work experience. As I mentioned earlier the biggest problem with university is there are thousands of other people with the same degree as you, meaning you need to stand out.

Placement years help you do that.

Therefore, I was very interested in them for that reason but as the years went by, I realised that there were two more reasons why I wanted to do a placement.

The first is a very personal reason because it meant I would be in education for another year, and it meant I would live at home rent free for another year.

I know I am extremely fortunate to have those circumstances and I do lots of chores anyway, so it isn't exactly rent-free, but I am extremely grateful.

Secondly, I wanted to do a placement because it would give me another year at university so I could figure out what I wanted. Because if you've read literally any of my other books then you know that I love psychology.

To me psychology is amazing and I will always defend psychology and people interested in psychology from people who disrespect, are hostile and think psychology people are time-wasters.

However, I still have no idea from I what to do in terms of my dissertation and on from there. Since I know I want to do clinical psychology but that's like saying you want to go on holiday.

There are plenty of options to choose from!

So I hope that this extra year will not only help me increase my work experience and employability, but give me time to figure out what I want for the next few years.

Additionally, and this is a massive thing for me to open admit so early in this book. I suppose I want my placement year to increase my confidence again.

Since I'll talk more about this in the reflections,

but in my first and second year my academic writing wasn't good. I know these psychology topics inside and out and all of my other books prove that.

But apparently I couldn't write it in an academic way or a way that was academic enough to please the markers. And of course because universities just assume you can write perfect academic essays from day one, there wasn't a lot of people to help me.

That's another thing I hope to get out of this placement, so this is a happy accident with the placement being an academic one.

And I just remembered a final reason, I want to use this placement to see what I enjoy doing. As I want to test the waters in the psychology job market to see what I directly want to do, explore and work in in later life.

As well as as I write this half way through my placement, I know I can safely say I am definitely learning this.

Overall, when it comes to doing a psychology placement, just ask yourself what you want to achieve and why you're doing it. Not only will this help you choose your placement, but it will help you get through the tough times, if you have any.

HOW DID I FIND A PLACEMENT?

Whilst this chapter is more aimed for students who are considering or trying to find out more about psychology placements, this chapter will still be interesting for everyone.

During my first two years of university (generally speaking), I didn't need to do anything else for my placement except make sure my overall marks stayed above 60 so it showed that I had the knowledge to go on placement.

However, in the second year of my degree, I needed to get the score of 60 at least as I mentioned above, but this is when you start to find out more about your placements and how it all worked.

Therefore, what happened to me was in the early October of my second year, there was a placement evening where the university explained to us how the placement works. Then a group of companies ranging from NHS mental health services to schools to businesses come in and give us a presentation.

Personally, I'm sure their presentations are meant to give us a broad look at what's available but basically the entire point of those presentations are the company is trying to sell themselves to us.

In other words they want the best placement students before anyone else gets them.

Then after that there are a number of students who have returned from their placement year and they talk about their experiences.

As I mentioned in the introduction of the book, I know most of what they're saying is very true, but equally you know that they will never say anything bad about the placement with the university standing in the same room as them.

So you will only ever hear good things about the placements.

However, my placement evening was online because it was during the pandemic, but yours will most probably be in-person. Therefore, an unofficial tip would be if you hear about a type of placement you enjoy and there's a student who spoke about it, go up to them and quietly ask if there was anything they didn't like about the placement.

I know most of the time there won't be anything negative or bad about the placement, but there might be and it helps to give you a fuller idea of the placement you want to look into.

After the placement evening, you need to start applying to placements. Thankfully my university already had a large list of placement ads from various companies that we could apply for.

Thus, always check out the ones on the university's page and apply for them and keep checking your emails as I got plenty of emails over the year about new opportunities as they were added.

Additionally, most of these application processes include sending in your CV (or your equivalent in your country), getting an interview and seeing if you get the job.

Yet I did have to do some basic maths and English tests as part of some application processes. But we're talking basic maths like 1+1 here, or something that simple.

Subsequently, after you have found your placement, you'll be required to email the university, tell them about it and then it will be a matter of filling out some easier paperwork. Due to the university still has Duty of Care over you whilst you are on your placement.

In other words, the university will still look after you and make sure you won't be harmed by the placement.

Lastly, there was a meeting for me around July were the university spoke to us, gave us some guidance and explained a few more things to us. But I must, must, must stress that you listen to this meeting, because as I was dead sure I wasn't going to get high enough marks to go on placement, I didn't take too much in.

Don't do what I did because if you think like this, you'll very surprised like I was to find out you were going on placement.

So definitely listen to that meeting just in case there is something important, and it's another chance to ask questions to the university.

What Happens If You Don't Get A Placement?

This is a question that lots of students are concerned about and it does cause them some stress.

But please don't be.

At the end of the day it doesn't matter if you get a placement or not, there are other ways to stand out to employers and don't get stressed out so much that it hurts. As amazing as placements can be, there are not worth that much stress.

Consequently, if you don't find a placement by a certain time, for me it was week 30 of the academic year, you won't be going on placement, instead you'll just transfer to a non-placement degree, and do your final year instead.

The same applies if you have a placement but don't get the required marks.

Now, I talk about this because I know for me I was concerned and worried about not getting a placement, and I don't want other students to have the same experience. I give a few more tips to help with that in the section below, but please internalise the fact that you won't fail your degree by not getting a placement. It only means you will do your final year a year earlier than you planned.

And there's nothing wrong with that.

My Other Tips:

Nevertheless, this is where we get into more honest territory and I add in a lot of my opinions.

Personally, I would have liked my university to actually give us more guidance on finding a placement because this did cause a lot of concern. Since they basically went to us, we've done your placement evening, now go off into the online world (or in-person) and find a placement.

They didn't offer us any tips or guides about finding them.

I suppose there were a few guides at the very bottom of the webpage with all the advertisements. But I still strongly believe they should have taken a more proactive approach to telling us about it.

In addition, as my university didn't tell me this, I'm going to be explaining it to you. When it comes to applying for placements, I highly recommend you apply for as many as you can.

As I was talking to different people on different placement degrees (like Law, Economics and more) and they said that they had applied for at least 30+ and there was still a high rate of rejection.

Putting this into practical terms for us, as far as I know there are only two universities in the UK as I write this that offers psychology placements. But I haven't looked in the North of England, Scotland, Wales or Northern Ireland, so there could be more.

Also you don't need to apply for as many as 30,

that was extreme I think. But it shows my point that you should try and apply for as many placements as possible, because you will be rejected.

I remember I applied for 9 placements.

I don't think that was enough and in all honesty, if I didn't apply for a certain academic placement the second it became available, I don't think I would be sitting here telling you about my placement.

Furthermore, if we break out my responses to my applications, 4 got back to me with rejects, 4 never replied and I only got one acceptance.

If you have more that is amazing but it won't happen for everyone.

Overall, please try and apply for as many placements as you can, don't stress yourself out about it, but you might want to cast a wide net as they said.

As well as I do slightly regret not being a bit more ambitious and applying for placement not in the Southeast of England as that did limit my options. Granted I only did that due to personal circumstances.

On the whole, my tips for psychology placements at the end of this chapter are apply for as many placements as your personal circumstances allow, and make sure you research them too, to make sure they are going to be something you're going to enjoy.

Saying that, I didn't think I would enjoy an academic placement, but I am.

THE FIRST REFLECTION

In the future, I really need to write these reflections on the day something interesting happens but as this was just my first week, this will be fine.

As well as considering how last week (20th September 2021) was meant to be the start of my placement, when my placement officially started I was thankfully surprised that the first week went as well as it did.

So all in all there are some things to reflect on that you too should find interesting.

<u>Monday Meeting</u>

After the chaos of last week because everything was very up in the air and I don't do up in the air. I like to be able to plan for things with some certainty so I was a little bit *stressed* about the lack of my placement.

Leading to up emails and thankfully we organised a meeting on Monday 27th September to discuss my placement.

Personally, at this point I had no idea what I was actually doing for my placement and I didn't even know if I was doing it from home or going into the university and working from there.

Again I was *stressed* that I was so in the dark.

However, in terms of reflecting, this uncertainty and being so kept in the dark, really did affect my interest and want to do this placement. I won't lie that's what I felt like.

So in case you ever feel like this, it's okay to feel nervous and anxious about your placement when you start or before you start. That probably means you're interested in the topic and want to do it.

In addition, at the meeting after some Skype troubles we switched to Teams (I think we'll all agree we'll be happier when we can see each other face to face again) and we got talking about the placement.

Leading to them telling me what my placement would be about. Of course this won't normally be a problem because most placements will tell you exactly what you'll be doing straight away when you sign up, so please don't be nervous about this.

Yet I was told but it changed for some reason and personally if I was doing this again I would make sure I knew or asked what I'll be doing when my placement started.

Back to the meeting, they said there would be two projects I'll be working on over the next year. The first one was strongly given to me and the second one I could choose.

Very interestingly, the first project was to complete a literature review on Mobile Mental Health Apps that their last placement student had started but never finished. Therefore, I would need to finish writing it, researching and create a reference list.

And the funny thing about this was, I had looked at her write-up before the meeting because it had been emailed to me and I thought it was 90% done.

It wasn't.

It really wasn't. But it was an interesting topic so that wasn't too much of a problem.

To reflect on the idea of my first project, it was great considering the entire point of my placement is to expand my psychological knowledge into areas that I haven't studied, and that's very true.

I have never looked at the effectiveness of Mental Health Apps as behavioural interventions and remembering how important these apps are and their relevance to our modern society. This sounds great and I know I'll be interested in the topic.

The only problem I had is I'll be going over someone else's work and using their words and notes and morphing it into a full literature review.

As I write that it sounds easier and when I get more into the review, I'm sure it will be because I'll have a better understanding of how she thinks and writes.

But at the moment, this is tricky because her voice (way her writes) is very different to me and the main problem I'm facing is: did she write that because it was her voice and she was writing a rough draft? Or did she write it because that's how your meant to write academically?

Which leads me to another point, because I've written probably over million (probably more) words of easy to understand and engaging nonfiction and fiction. This means I can write engaging books that people love and enjoy, but it makes academic writing a bit more difficult. I can write good essays but my academic writing can be improved.

Hopefully, my placement year can help with that as well as I can talk about it with my placement supervisor and his PhD student.

For you, if you're thinking about doing a placement at a university but you're concerned about your academic writing. There are two things you need to bear in mind.

The first is wherever you do your placement you will need to do some form of academic writing because you'll need to do a project or some kind of coursework.

Secondly (and this paragraph is more for my benefit), if you're on a placement then you got good grades overall. It doesn't matter if your average academic writing only allowed you to scrap pass the mark you needed for your placement year.

You still got the mark so you deserve to be on your placement and see your placement year as a way to improve your academic writing.

Then what happened for that project was there

was a handover meeting with the Placement Student from last year which was good. Since she explained her… bad notes and it cleared up what her thinking and the references.

Personally, she didn't do her referencing how I liked to do it because when I write an essay or an academic piece, I always collect my references and create a rough bibliography (Sorry APA 7th Edition I mean Reference List!) as I go.

But she pasted links and odd citations without any references so I spent two hours on Wednesday creating a rough reference list just to clear up her draft review. It looked really messy with all the links!

Afterwards on Thursday, I researched how to write a review properly, I read the review my Supervisor and Placement student did so I understand how to write it. Then I did the introduction of my review.

The Second Project:

Subsequently, the second project I'll be doing after the literature review was a choice between two potential projects.

The first was a project that involved creating a social media use scale that measured certain aspects of behaviours and this was in my placement supervisor's planning tasks.

Since my Supervisor and his PhD student did a recent literature review about the pros and cons of social media use on depression, mental health and as a sense of communities.

As well as what I understood from their brief explanation was they found certain types of behaviours were predictors of certain social media outcomes, both positive and negative.

As a result, the social media scale would be designed to measure these predictors. Then we would conduct a study to test the scale and do some kind of advance statistics to see if the scale worked.

Of course, you all know I don't talk about advance statistics in these books but that's the jest of what was going to happen with that option.

That was the option I choose.

Moreover, the second option was just in the brainstorming stage as they put it because they wanted to look at how discipline and strictness in school affected mental health down the line.

On paper this sounds really interesting and I would have liked to pursue this but the question that instantly popped into my mind was: how do you test it?

Considering in late 2021, access to schools is restricted and 2022 I doubt will be too much better at the moment and I can't manipulate the variables so an experiment is off the table.

Also they suggested self-reported data but that's extremely flawed in this situation because in my experience as a secondary (High) school student is as soon as a teacher tells a student off for breaking a rule around school uniform. The student instantly shouts and screams and can't believe how strict the school is.

When in reality, my school was hardly stricted compared to other schools that my other friends went to.

Thus, how you would test this reliably is beyond me.

<u>Reflection of Option 1:</u>

The reason why I wanted to do the first option was mainly because it was the best option and they asked if there was anything that I wanted to research.

And truth be told, I am terrified of my final year at University because there isn't a topic I feel drawn to, to do my dissertation on.

Read any of my other books and you'll see I absolutely love psychology and especially clinical, social, forensic and personality psychology. I love them all but to study them… I don't feel the drive to study them for a year.

Of course, I'll have to but I wanted to mention this in case that helped other students to feel less alone if they feel the same way.

In addition, when I thought about it more, I did choose the first option for a few other reasons. For example, it was an interesting topic and possibly with career and further education benefits. Since this involves some advance statistics and if the scale actually works then that's impressive to be a part of a research group that developed a new tool.

Possibly making my application to future jobs and universities better and stand out more.

Also it's a great way to really expand on my

statistics knowledge far beyond what I leant in class and I'll probably reflect on it at some point during this book.

On the flip side, I'm not sure there are any negatives (for the moment) because creating a social media use does sound interesting and challenging and I do like a challenge.

All in all I am looking forward to this.

University Paperwork:

Now I know this might not sound like the most exciting subtitled section but I think this is important for placement students to understand.

The University still has duty of care over you whilst you're on your placement.

Meaning the University will look after you and make sure your health and safety aren't harmed by your placement.

Which I was reminded of this week because I was meant to email the School of Psychology's Placement team when I officially started my placement. This was meant to be last week but of course I didn't email them.

Leading to an email this week from them asking me if I had started yet, so I confirmed I started on the 27th September and they sent me some paperwork.

The first form was a work from home form, the second was a Placement Agreement which me and my Placement Supervisor had to sign then the last form was something for my Supervisor.

All in all, I felt like this was important to mention

because I know I felt at the beginning of this placement process, I was a bit concerned I was going to be alone. As well as I wouldn't have the university behind me.

But in my experience nothing could be further from the truth because at my university the placement people were wonderful and really friendly. Which we can all agree is great considering whenever we email lectures and university people, the emails are always unfriendly and overly professional.

So if you take anything away from this section, please know the University will support you before, during and after your placement. You are far from alone at your placement.

A WEEK OF IMPROVEMENT, LEARNING AND A MAJOR GOOGLE SCHOLAR TRICK

With the completion of my second week at my placement, I have to admit I'm surprised that there are things to reflect. Since I doubted I'll have anything major to reflect this week.

But I do and both you and me can learn a lot from this week.

Overview:

I know some of you like to know exactly what I've been up to then I'll reflect more on the lessons learnt later on.

Therefore, on the first two days of this week, I was proofreading and adding to the 6 sections the placement student before me wrote up. That was easy and it didn't take me very long.

Then for the last two days of this week, I started

to write my three sections of the review which I'll reflect on below because something interesting happened.

Overall, I am enjoying this placement because on the whole the work is easy. As well as the work is very interesting because I've learnt a lot about mHealth apps and how they affect mental health and they could even be used as mental health interventions.

Improvement In Academic Writing:

I'm famously bad for my academic writing, give me a fiction book or psychology nonfiction to write and I can write it very well. But academic writing is something I've always struggled with to some extent because of the tight structure, being concise and the massive words you have to use. I'm not talking about psychology terminology, I'm talking about words like *judiciously* where normally I would use a few extra words to say the same.

Part of this is just down to how I get paid in fiction because you get paid by word count. But all in all academic is a bit tricker for me. I get good grades but improving is very difficult I've found.

So if you struggle with academic writing you aren't alone!

However, I wanted to reflect on this because I now have a major tip that should help you improve your own. Due to in week 1 of my placement I read a 10,000+ word of a literature review and thought nothing more of it.

Yet when I started to write up sections of this

literature review, I realised my academic writing had improved and that all came from reading a literature review.

Therefore, I know to you this doesn't sound exciting or interesting, but read academic papers. As well as if you read ones on topics you're interested about then this makes it fun and interesting.

I cannot recommend reading papers enough. It does improve your academic writing. Of course, your mileage may vary but still. It worked for me so I hope it does for you.

Also I never ever would have said this two years ago when I first started university but I think I will make myself read academic papers more from time to time. So the academic style and word choices can sink in.

Google Scholar Trick:

I really wanted to add this section because I found this great shortcut on Google Scholar this week that I have to share.

So you're on Google Scholar and you've found an online article. You click on the article, it's great, it's perfect for what you need. But it doesn't have a citation button or it does but it isn't in APA format.

What do you do?

You need to click back to the article on Google Scholar then they'll be a " button. Click it and it'll bring up the article reference/ citation in APA and other formatting.

This is such a brilliant time saver. Once you

check out Google Scholar you'll see what I mean but that trick has saved me so much time this week!

A Massive Article:

Something I'm finding weird about these reflections and all of the reflective type psychology books I write is how honest I am in them. This shouldn't really be a surprise I am honest in all my books but these reflective books I find I'm extremely honest, so much so I feel naked on the page.

This next section proves it.

In addition, to my poorer academic writing, I am also somewhat poor on the idea of the big article and using it in your essay.

Let me explain.

I once remember asking my friend for a copy of this essay for a past assignment so I could learn his structure and what he did. Bearing in mind, at this point I tended to get 55s for my essays and he tends to get 80+. So asking him for help was a no brainer.

Note: as always nothing in this book is an official tip or advice from me to you.

Thus, I got his essay, looked at the structure and everything. But something that I realised was he found one major review article and he used that to studies and references for the rest of his essay. Resulting in him having like 20-40 references at the end of his essay.

I put what I learnt to use and I managed to push my essay grades up to a 58 which I was gutted by because I thought I would do better than that and get

60+.

Anyway, I was writing up a section on mHealth apps and music using the last placement's students notes and one of her references was a large(ish) literature review on music and mHealth apps. But what I found interesting were the rest of her notes were made from this one article.

For me this was amazing because it meant all I had to do was write up her notes and add the citations and references as required.

Consequently, to reflect on this probably, I think when I'm in my final year and I'm given an essay topic. I'll try and find a literature review or something similar to it then I'll try and use it to form my essay.

I think this could be a good idea because the literature review would already have a structure so I can adapt them. It already has TONS of references and every little thing is already referenced for you.

This was always a source of annoyance for me because I would write something, maybe a sentence or two, that I had heard from a lecturer, read something and more. But I wouldn't be able to find a citation so the university markers would moan at me.

Not ideal!

However, with my finding out about this literature review method or whatever you want to call it. I think this will definitely help me write better essays.

Conclusion:

At this point in time I want to say that I am really

enjoying my placement and I am learning new things that will help me in the future. Since with my academic writing improving then I hope I can write better essays, get higher grades and do better in my degree.

Also in all honesty, I do have massive doubts about doing my PhD because I want to do it. I just doubt my academic writing will be good enough to do it but I am starting to think this might not be true now.

Overall, I hope I keep improving and this is why I encourage students to do a placement year if you have the opportunity because you will learn so much. I've learnt tons in the first two weeks of my placement that will benefit me in the future.

Finally, I know an academic placement doesn't sound exciting and that's what I thought in the beginning. Although now I know and can see my improvement, I'm really glad I have the opportunity to do an academic placement and work on academic projects.

So whatever you decide for your placement, I know you'll learn lots and should have lots of fun doing it!

FOMO ON PLACEMENTS

At first I honestly believed there would be nothing to reflect on this week, and at least in terms of my placement that's true. But something strange happened that I need to reflect on because I know I am far from the only one who this affects.

Therefore, I have never been a person who gets affected my FOMO (Fear of Missing Out), as a child if there was new game that people loved, a new book that the world was praising and screaming over and a new TV programmes that I couldn't watch. I basically couldn't care less.

Even as an author there are lots of trends and fades that I don't follow. Simply because I know they're fades and crazies, as well as soon something else will come along and the old thing will disappear.

All in all, I am not a FOMO person and I'm guessing there are plenty of other people like me.

However, as part of my placement, my placement

supervisor strongly recommend I become more proactive on LinkedIn. You know the social networking site for people in suits and professionals.

Before my placement, I had created an account, filled in my profile a little and I post the newest episode of The Psychology World Podcast on there every Monday. Besides from that, I don't use it. Since I'm as author I know social media does not sell books so I would rather use social media time to write more, connect with readers and do more university work.

Nonetheless, my placement supervisor wanted me to take LinkedIn more seriously because it would benefit my future making all these connections.

I didn't have the heart to tell him I completely disagreed.

Anyway, every Monday (but now Sunday because I realise LinkedIn works on the calendar week, not working week) I have gone onto LinkedIn, typed in Psychology and I've been maxing out my connections each week.

A better analogy for you might be, I've joined sending friend requests each week to 100 people, as that's the limit on LinkedIn.

The FOMO:

This week I went onto LinkedIn because my phone had been going mad with notifications, and like you do I started to scroll. Thus, I kept seeing lots and lots of people on their placements, enjoying it, getting to work and interact with people and doing "proper" placements.

As well as I didn't realise it at the time until I was having a random conversation with someone that it dawned on me that I was suffering from FOMO.

Due to I was seeing all these psychology students on their placement, working in Hospitals and real clinical psychology settings, and having a great time.

In addition, it probably didn't help that I had applied to tons of clinical psychology placements in the South East of England and London. I applied for some with dementia services, psychological interventions for Cleft Lip and older people services.

But I didn't get any.

Resulting in me probably feeling like a bit of a failure and nowhere near as successful as other students.

<u>Over To You:</u>

Whether you're on your placement or not, I have no doubt you will experience this at some point, and I can promise you if I had got a hospital placement. I probably would still experience FOMO about someone placement position.

Therefore, I do truly believe that these are perfectly normal feelings and if you do or have felt like this on your placement. It doesn't necessarily mean you've made a wrong decision, you've messed up and all the other negative things you'll be thinking of.

Instead it just means you're human. A perfectly normal human that wants to experience other things and develop themselves in psychology.

That's definitely a reason why I experienced FOMO, because I knew if I got a clinical psychology placement in a hospital then that would benefit me. As I would have real life practical experience that jobs and PhD programs love.

How I Got Over FOMO?

Going back to the conversation I was having, the person I was talking to helped me to realise, I was perfectly happy with my placement. Because it's extremely flexible at the moment, I get to do the hours I want, I have minimal supervision. Since I just email a weekly progress report on the work and that's it.

In fact as I write this, I emailed a finished version of the literature review to my PhD student I work with so he can review it, check it and suggest improvements.

As well as this placement gives me time to do what I love. Which is write nonfiction, fiction, I get to read about psychology, I can podcast and I get to do so many things I love.

All whilst doing my placement.

I couldn't do that if I was at a hospital placement doing 9 til 5.

Overall, I know this is just my experience and of course your placement will be different. But FOMO is natural and it's nothing to be ashamed of.

To wrap up this chapter, all I can say is, if you're looking or thinking about a placement at the moment. Apply for as many as you can and as many ones you really, really want to do. You need to have fun and be interested in your placement for that year, so pick a good one.

If you're on your placement year now, if you ever feel FOMO, just focus on the positives and how amazing your placement is. There will be negative times, times where you're stressed, bored and believe you're wasting your life. But focus on the positives because it will all help you in the future.

THE PICKINESS AND PRETTINESS OF ACADEMIA AND TIPS AND HOPE

I have no doubt there are going to be some students who think I'm blasphemous towards the golden, divine rules of academia.

However, this chapter does give you plenty of tips to help improve your own academic writing.

Personally, if that's your opinion then I have little doubt you couldn't do extremely well at university. But I'm not writing for these great students, I'm writing and talking to average students who probably hate the silly rules of academia just as much as me.

Therefore, I intended not to write a reflection this week because all I was doing where some improvements to my literature review, so I hardly expected to have any of interest to reflect on.

However, when I got my improvements back, there were some improvements or suggestions that I looked at and was thinking, seriously? Does that actually matter?

For example, we all know that if you have four or more (now three or more because of APA 7th Edition) authors on a paper, you need to add *et al* onto the citation. Such as if the paper was Andrew, Whiteley, Cherryman, Sinks and Poppy (2020). Then you would shorten this Andrew et al (2020)

What's wrong with that?

Now I can guess that you've one of two responses. The first is my response: what's he talking about? There's nothing wrong with that? Or the some of you mind of had the second one: *Oh My God I'm reading a book by a person who clearly knows nothing about citations!*

Since you need a full stop to the end of et al for it to be correct.

Therefore, the correct way to cite our example was Andrew et al. (2020). And that's what I meant the pettiness of academia because if you looked at that reference it would mean the exact same thing with or without the full stop.

Therefore I did laugh about some of the suggestions.

Tip 1:

In academic writing, always add a full stop to the et al part of a citation.

Tip 2:

In a larger piece of academic writing like a literature review, don't start sections with however and similar words. Since my placement supervisor told me sections need to be standalone.

Tip 3:

If you have two authors, it's *&*, not *and*. For instance, it's *Andrew & Whiteley (2020),* not *Andrew and Whiteley (2020).*

In all fairness I did know that, but I sent my literature review to him before it was formatted because I wanted him to focus on my suggestions for improving the content, not the formatting.

Luckily, there were barely any content suggestions.

Tip 4:

With my background mainly being in professional fiction writing and I write easy-to-understand and engaging nonfiction, this next tip was difficult for me to grasp. But it's academic writing so quite literally anything goes.

Your paragraphs should be between 150-250 words long, this isn't always the case but this is the ideal length. As well as please don't ask me why, because my answer will probably be: *it's academia just go with it.*

Reflection:

Despite me having a lot of laughter this week at the pettiness of academia and all the little (pointless) rules of academic writing, this has still been a good week.

It's allowed me to improve my *academic* writing skills and keep learning about the rules and silliness that goes along with it. Also at least I doubt I'll have the constant feedback on my essays now that criticise my citations.

And that's another point I hate about university feedback, they criticise you but they don't offer good explanations to help you improve!

Anyway, this placement is good for me and hopefully my future, at least in academia.

Over To You:

If you're considering doing your own placement, then hopefully this week has shown you that placements can really help you improve your knowledge, and it helps you for the future. For me it helped with my academic writing, for you (depending on your placement) it could help you with writing, confidence, speaking, dealing with other people and many more great skills you'll need for the future world of psychology!

If you're currently working on a placement, then I really hope this week has shown you that sometimes you will get feedback that is silly and pointless. As well as sometimes you know feedback won't help you with your future ambitions.

However, I hope that after reading this chapter, I hope everyone can see that placements are a great time for learning and developing as a person and as a professional. And sometimes feedback is a key part of that.

WEEK 10 REFLECTION

I have to admit it has been a while since I last did a reflection, it's been at least six weeks, because I've been busy with the placement and the other things I do outside of university life.

However, now I realise I really need to do a series of reflections, so the point of this chapter will be to catch you up on what's been happening and then I'll reflect on this to.

In addition, I suppose the first reflection is I highly recommend you do what the university tells you in regards to the coursework. For example, my university told us clearly that for the first week of our placement, we should do daily reflections then after that we need to be doing weekly reflections.

I started off doing that.

I fell off the wagon (so to speak) after week four of the placement, so I highly recommend you do stick your university's guidelines about your coursework. Since Fridays are my days off my placement because that's the day I'm meant to be doing my university coursework.

However, because I have podcasts and other things to do, I've had a terrible habit of not even trying to do my coursework unless I think there is something major to reflect on.

All in all, in the future I will try to do more reflections as part of my coursework.

<u>Learning More About Academic Writing</u>

Something major that has been happening in the past few weeks is my academic writing is really improving because of this placement. For example, all the little things I spoke about in the week 4 reflection are becoming reinforced and every draft I get back from my supervisor is allowing me to build upon my knowledge even further.

Some of the improvements or things I now know include:

- Whenever you do any sort of academic writing, always go back through and condense it.
- When referring to reviews just put (for review(s) see, *insert reference(s)*)
- Always write an introduction in past tense

Also another tip about writing an introduction to an academic report is always go to town on justifying why your study is needed. It's always better to overdo the justification and cut it out later, then underdo it and no one cares about your research. Because they don't see it as important to and it doesn't fill any gaps in the literature.

Then here are some other points I've learnt for a general overview of a literature review:

- It's a roadmap for the rest of the review.
- Start with earliest research then summarise up to the latest.
- Then say your aim or direction for the review.

I have learnt lots of other things but hopefully you found some of those points useful.

Therefore, I'm really pleased with my progress as I can see myself improving and I know this will benefit me for years to come, not only in my last year or university but in my Masters and PhD as well.

As a result, if you want to do an academic placement, I still think there is no shame in it because whilst you might not think of it as a "proper" clinical psychology placement, it could still be extremely useful to you.

I know that without this placement, my academic writing would still be as bad as it was in my second year.

So that is something to consider when you're looking for placement- what do you want to get back out of it?

On the other hand, if you are already a placement student then I want you to know that it's okay for your academic writing not to be great and you should use your placement to improve upon it, if you're doing an academic placement.

Back To University Days

Of course, I can't know what your university calls these days but my university calls them "Back To INSERT UNIVERSITY NAME Days" and the entire point of these days is for you to check with the university and them to make sure you're finding your placement okay, you're doing things and you're learning.

Now as I write this, today was meant to be my Back To University Day, which I was looking forward to and not looking forward to for a few reasons.

The main reason why I was looking forward to it was because it would give me a chance to see other students, get to hear about their placements and just tap into the university experience a little more.

In addition, it would have been great to be able to talk to the placement people at the university about the coursework requirements. Since it dawned on me this week (after reading a few university emails) that I don't think I'm doing the coursework correctly.

I'm not talking about the reflective part of the coursework.

Instead I'm talking about the project part because even though I am doing projects on my academic placement, I don't think they would meet the requirements for the coursework as I haven't submitted my study (or the study I'm a part of) for ethical approval.

Therefore, that is something I need to investigate

next week and find out what the requirements are for the coursework.

In terms of reflecting on this, personally I would have preferred the university to be a bit more transparent in regards to what they needed from us. Because all they're done is uploaded the information onto our Module webpage and didn't even tell us it was loaded up until later in the term.

What would have been ideal and I think they were planning on this but they didn't get around to it, was to have a zoom meeting with all of us to explain the coursework.

But it didn't happen.

Nevertheless, I am an independent learner so it wouldn't hard for me to find out the requirements and do what's needed. I just hope it won't be massive amounts of work for me to catch up.

Consequently, my advice for both placement and looking-for-a-placement students is to look at your coursework requirements at the beginning of your placement, make a list of what's required and basically create an action plan.

But more on my experience in the next reflection.

Meeting People

Before we move onto what I've actually been doing during my placement, I want to stress to you that your placement is a great opportunity to meet new people with amazing stories, backgrounds and interests.

What I mean is because my placement is of course an academic one with my placement supervisor being a lecturer, he has numbers of students that he supervises from final year students to masters to PhD students.

Meaning he organises socials from time to time so everyone can meet each other, talk, make friends, etc.

So one of these socials happened a few weeks ago and I want to mention it for two main reasons.

Firstly, socials are great fun. We played games, did some great ice breakers, had some food and it was great to see other people about my age with similar interests and university experiences.

Therefore, if you ever get to go to a university social (at least one organised by an academic) then I highly recommend you go because it should be great. As well as it won't be as bad as you think.

Leading me onto my second reason, because I was… really, really nervous about going to it. Due to from everything I've heard about university socials, I thought they were all about drinking, clubbing and all the typical university things that I don't like.

So I was nervous about going.

Yet I went to the social and had a great time, it was fun, enjoyable and great to hear about other people.

Two of my favourite things were the ice breaker called 2 truths and a lie. I cannot recommend that enough because someone had some interesting truths and things that happened to them, so definitely play that if you can.

Then my second favourite thing was I was brilliant at the Pictionary game we played as no one else wanted to try to be Pictionary with the Milgram studies and the Stanford Prison Experiment. But I tried them and everyone was really impressed that I could do them and people understood them.

So that was a win.

All in all, regardless of whatever placement you want to pick or are doing right now, try and take advantage of the socials. You never know what's going to happen, the fun you'll have and it might be exactly what you needed.

I know for me I really did need that social and I'm glad I went.

Additional Learning Opportunities

I'll reflect on the two major things I've been doing in the next reflection, but I wanted to explain another benefit of placements that I didn't even know about.

As sometimes when you're on your placement, you get to attend additional learning opportunities.

For instance I have heard that some placement students working in mental health settings get to go to conferences and other major learning opportunities with their supervisors. Which I think sounds amazing and I would love to go to one of them in the future.

Nevertheless, for me the additional learning opportunity popped up recently because my

Placement Supervisor's PhD student (I know I really need to give these people pseudonyms) is doing a bit of teaching at the university to help fund some of his PhD.

As a result, next week as I write this, he has a one-on-one lesson with one of his students on Exploratory Factor Analysis which he invited me to.

This was very nice for him to invite me and I would have quite liked to go, because it would have helped my understanding better about one of the topics we're doing. But I can't attend because of complex(ish) travel I would have to do so early in the morning.

Yet if it was even an hour later in the day I would have gone.

However, the entire point of this is to show you a great benefit of a placement is the learning opportunities that will mostly certainly pop up without you knowing.

Therefore, when these opportunities do pop up, I really suggest that you do take a good look at them.

For example, the opportunity I was offered on Exploratory Factor Analysis, it was for one hour on a topic I would probably never use again. But I still wanted to go because it was a bit of extra learning.

Yet it was the travel and time that made it a bit unfeasible.

On the other hand, if I was invited to a attend a conference in London (which is only half an hour away on the high speed train) that I probably would attend to. Because the travel would be worth it because there are major learning, networking and other opportunities at conferences.

So for me, it would be worth it.

But you're a different person.

Overall, if you are ever presented with any additional learning opportunity, look at it, reflect on it and see if it would benefit you.

Then decide if you want to take advantage of it.

PERSONAL AND PROFESSIONAL DEVELOPMENT SO FAR AND OTHER NOTE WORTHY MENTIONS

On the day I write this, I decided to finally check out the webpage dedicated to my placement and its coursework on my university's website. As well as whilst I'll talk more about why I did this in another reflection, I read a critical component of my reflection coursework was I needed to consider how these things have helped me grow personally and professionally.

Therefore, I'll explain both these points using my own experiences then I'll apply these to you throughout and at the end of the reflection.

<u>Professional Growth</u>

This is always easier to think about because the entire point of doing a placement is professional development. Meaning you meet new people, learn new skills and expand your knowledge

For me and my placement, I definitely think I have grown professionally in a few key areas.

Academic Writing Improvement

One of which for me was massive, that was the area of academic writing, because you're reading this book and you might have read my other books, blogs or basically everything where I write about nonfiction topics.

You should have noticed that all of these are written in an engaging, fun and personal way. Nothing like academic writing.

Overall, I have written almost half a million words over the years of engaging, easy to understand nonfiction.

This is great for everything except university. Since all this nonfiction training means I don't get on well with academic writing.

In addition, most of you will probably agree with me that at university we are not taught how to write academically. Sure there are workshops, online materials and more, but they aren't helpful. At least in my experience.

As a result, I can know a topic inside and out for an essay, an assignment or exam. But because I can't write academically to their standards, I never get very high marks. No matter how much I try.

So this was definitely a major advantage of this placement because it allowed me to work with real academics doing real research and they told me how to improve.

As that is another annoying thing about university, I think we can all agree on. We hardly ever get useful feedback on how to improve in our assignments.

However, I will mention that I do understand the other side because two nights ago (as I write this) I was at a university social and we were talking about this topic exactly.

It turns out that lecturers and everyone else who marks our assignments only get paid for 40 minutes per 3,000 word assignment.

Of course in reality it takes longer than 40 minutes but they don't get paid for it, so the question is for markers: why spend extra time giving feedback when it makes them loose money?

And universities wonder why lectures and people go on strike…

Anyway, all in all, this placement has been great for me because I can see an improvement in my academic writing that will hopefully help me in my final year of undergraduate and hopefully in future postgraduate programmes.

In terms of you, if you want to work in academia and/or want to improve your academic writing, then you might want to think about an academic placement.

Personally, I was skeptical about how much I would enjoy it and if it would be worth my time, I think it is and I really have enjoyed it so far.

It's something to consider.

Experience In Research and Reports

Regardless of what type of placement you choose, I definitely thing is a universal because you almost certainly would have to do a research project and write up a research report.

In terms of professional development, this is great because not only will it help you to improve your report writing, research skills and deepen your knowledge about research in the real world. But it will give you critical skills that will help you in your final year.

I will comment directly or indirectly in another reflection on this point, because this far in my placement I have completed a literature review and we're starting a social media study.

Both of these have been great for me because it's allowed me to improve my academic writing. But more importantly it has allowed me to develop a deeper understanding of how professional literature reviews and research is done.

Meaning I can easily use this knowledge next year for my dissertation.

On the whole, if you want to work in academia or what I talk about in the section below, I would seriously consider an academic placement.

A Note On Finding Your Interests In higher Education:

Now I want to go off on a minor tangent here, because people who are doing academic placements will probably agree here, I'm finding out a lot about my attitudes towards more advance degrees during this placement.

Since as I've mentioned before I'm working with a wonderful PhD student and I'm meeting Masters and other PhD students through the university socials, and I am starting to find that I probably do not have the interest in academia to do some of these advance degrees.

For example, do NOT take my word for it but what I have understood about PhDs is a lot of other things involved that aren't related to your project. As well as your project from what I hear is about 100,000 words.

And my view is if I am struggling to write 2,000 words of professional academic writing now, how am I meant to do 50x times?

Nevertheless I should note I want to do a Clinical Psychology Doctorate and that has a completely different training program as you have to go out and do your four placements.

So that was all far, far, far from official advice, but an academic placement could be useful in helping you understand your feelings towards academia as a whole.

Personal Development

In all honesty, I don't think there is a lot of personal development that I can mention here because none of it is that obvious.

The only personal development I can think of is

I am happier meeting new people now. I still prefer smaller groups of people but I am more than happy to meet new ones after this placement.

Since I have had to on these university socials and it is really good to hear everyone's different experiences, stages and interests.

It surprised me that I like these socials as much as I do.

For both prospective and current placement students, as I've said before if your placement environment offers a social or something similar, you do need to consider it because it can be great fun and useful to you.

Conclusion:

To wrap up this reflection I want to stress that doing a placement (whatever it is) has so many great benefits that you would not get if you just stuck with a normal degree.

With your placement, you will grow personally and professionally as well as that will benefit you in the future, so I do recommend them.

For students who are on their placement, I hope you're enjoying them and feeling your own growth.

Just know that this growth will benefit you for years to come.

WHAT HAVE I DONE FOR MY PLACEMENT: MHEALTH LITERATURE REVIEW

The next two chapters will be on what are the main projects I've been doing for my placement, and most important I'll be reflecting on what I've learnt amongst other things.

Now I know I've mentioned them in passing in other reflections but I want to reflect upon them in more detail. So you can see some of the possible things you could be doing on your academic placement, if you choose to do one of course.

Therefore, in this reflection, I'll be focusing on my mHealth literature review.

This was my first project on my placement which I inherited from last year's placement student where she had done the majority of the research and made notes. Yet she hadn't written it up or done references.

Personally, I learnt very quickly that I prefer to work as I always have, research and write it as I go. Then create a list of references and cite within the text as I go. Not leave it to the end, so in a way this was very validating in my opinion.

In addition, the mHealth review was all about Mobile Mental Health apps and how they could be used to improve lives both as an individual use and as part of a treatment programme designed by a professional.

I know I learnt a lot from this literature review, least of all how to improve my academic writing which I've spoken about in previous reflections, but not about the topic as a whole.

Since mobile mental heath apps… it isn't a topic I would investigate by myself either in a book, my own time or on my podcast, because it isn't something that jumps out at me as interesting.

However, this is the great thing about placements, they get/ heavily direct you in a certain direction so you have to explore things that you wouldn't normally look at. Which is great because the placement topics are often really interesting so you don't might getting pushed in one direction.

For me, I was given two options with me being asked to recommend something I wanted to look at. But I don't know. I don't know what I'm interested at the moment enough to research.

Therefore, I choose the best option out of the two I was given for another project, which was the

Social Media Study that I'll talk about in the next reflection.

But the point is during your placement you will probably be given interesting topics to look at, at least in academic placements.

Then for more practical placements (like working in a clinical psychology setting), you will probably be given some interesting cases to work on, so get to develop your practical skills quicker.

Going back to looking at my mHealth review, I had no idea what I wanted to learn from it at the beginning because to me the placement was so new, I didn't know what to expect.

However, I am really glad that I did it, listened to everything that was mentioned as a possible improvement because I feel like I have learnt a lot.

<u>Over To You</u>

For you, I want to mention that if you're going to be starting a placement (and other on placement students can back me up here) it is perfectly natural to be nervous, concerned and maybe even anxious about your placement.

As you're going to be mixing and thrown into an environment that university doesn't actually prepare us for, so it's okay to be nervous.

But you need to embrace your placement, listen and enjoy it.

I was nervous at the start of mine but I embraced it, tried to learn as much as I could and now that I am half way through it, I have learnt so much. And I know I am only going to learn more.

<u>Conclusion:</u>

The entire point of this reflection was to highlight something you could be given or do if you end up doing an academic placement.

My doing a literature review it allowed me to research a brand new topic in depth, deepen my overall psychology knowledge and improve my academic writing amongst other things.

There are a lot of benefits to literature reviews and in case you thought what I did when I first started, I promise you literature reviews aren't boring, plain or a waste of time.

As with everything, it is only as boring as you think it is.

So I want to finish up this reflection by saying, whenever placement you end up, or are, doing embrace all the opportunities it gives you. Because if you do then you could be surprised by the amount of things you learn.

I know I was.

SOMETHING ANNOYING AND THE SOLUTION FOR YOU

Taking a momentary break from the look at the projects, a few reflections ago I mentioned that I was having to find out more about the coursework side of my placement, because as I said before I need to do a research project as part of the coursework. But as I have an academic placement, I'm hoping that I can use what I am already working on as the coursework.

Otherwise I am in massive trouble.

Since for the research project part of the coursework, you need to get ethical approval, conduct the study and then write up a report.

However, I was extremely unfortunate in two aspects. The first was that I completely forgot about it until I started thinking about the coursework a few reflections ago.

Yet the second aspect was during your

placement, you'll have back to university days, but my one got cancelled, because of the strikes. Which is problematic because that the day we were meant to find out more about the research projects and how to go about it.

Now, you might assume and logically believe that after the strikes the university people might email us, rearrange the day or in some way tell us what we would have covered on that day.

No.

No we didn't, not in the slightest.

Also bear in mind I have not had a single email from the university whatsoever over the last few months, not a check in, not anything.

I did understand this because it must be difficult to manage all the placement students, and I cannot fault them on that. But I was at least expecting a little more contact.

Anyway, going back to my main problem, I know I needed to ask the university about using the projects I am doing largely independently as part of my placement for my coursework.

Who would you ask first?

Firstly, I asked the psychology placement department, so they're wonderful on so many things and I do like the people there. But they were less than useful on this occasion, because they sent me to my academic supervisor.

Now, I do not speak to my supervisor often. In my three years (including my placement year) of being at university, I think I have optionally spoken to him once and he was not useful. As the massive problem with academics is when you ask them an academic question they completely forget what it was like to be a student, so they explain it like they're talking to another doctor or professor and not a student.

I know other supervisors are amazing, but mine was not.

Anyway, so I emailed him, explain that the placement people send me to him and he doesn't understand why because he can't help me.

Instead he sends me to the Director of the psychology placement department.

Therefore, as I write this little reflection, I am waiting on an email back from the Director. I'll be sure to tell you what happens next because the entire point of this book is to give you an accurate and honest account of my placement experience.

<u>My Advice To You</u>

My biggest piece of advice is definitely keep in contact with your university and know whenever you have a question, contact them. At the end of the day, they have Duty of Care over you, and 99% of the time they are amazing.

Additionally, I highly, highly recommend you know exactly what you're meant to do for the coursework side of the placement as soon as possible.

Therefore, unlike me, a few days after you have your placement confirmed (this is normally once you've found out you have passed your second year with enough marks to move onto the placement), I would go onto your module's webpage and look at everything.

Read through it all and if you have any questions, no matter how small, I would email the placement department and ask them to clarify whatever you need.

Because 99% of them will be more than happy to help you, so always take advantage of it.

THE NEW YEAR SO FAR

Something that I highly, highly recommend when it comes to your placement, is to do your reflective diary a lot more frequently than I have. Since I know at some point I will have to become rather militant about doing reflective entries once or even twice a week.

In fact that is what I need to start doing now.

Therefore, my tip is if you have to do a reflective diary as part of your placement coursework, do actually do it! Don't be like me and having to panic from time to time about not doing it. Do your entries as you go so you don't need to back date them as far back as I do.

And just to prove my bad point, I'm writing this in the second week of February and I've been doing things for my placement since Christmas.

What I did over the Christmas Break:

Therefore, over the Christmas break I was set the

task of reviewing literature for our next project, and the project itself sounds really interesting, because it's on serious games for autistic people.

These serious games are the educational games that are apparently specially designed to help autistic children learn critical skills for functioning in the world. Now I say apparently because the reason for the literature review is the evidence base for these serious games could be considered dodgy at best, and that's why we need to investigate it.

As a result, over the Christmas break, my job was to spend an hour a week (it was the Christmas university break after all) going through over 2,000 academic papers for relevancy.

In all fairness, I made it sound a lot worse than it actually was because all I had to do was read the title, abstract and indicate with a y or n, if the paper was relevant to our investigation. As well as because my placement supervisor had been working on this from time to time over the past few years, the earlier research papers were already looked at.

But still, I probably had to look at over 1,500 papers.

Over To You: Academic Placements

If you end up doing an academic placement, it is perfectly reasonable to imagine you would have to do something like this, but this is why placements are great to see if you want to work in this sort of environment.

Also this is as far as from bad I could have it, I

looked at all of these papers in just over 4 hours spread over 4 weeks.

Of course, in your placement setting, you will properly will not have 4 weeks, but it was one of the easiest 4 hours of my life, because you just scanned the title and abstract looking for keywords. Like I searched for autism, serious games, toys or games.

And I have to admit, some of the papers will make you laugh because I'm sure academics type in their keywords into a datasbase and just download a spreadsheet of all the papers. It was that spreadsheet that I was given.

Due to I had papers looking at Genetics, farming and geography. None of which was even remotely related to what I was investigating.

That did make me laugh.

<u>Over To You: Other Placement Settings</u>

In addition, if you don't choose an academic setting, there is still an important point to learn here, because at some point in your academic life (most probably your third year at university for your dissertation), you will have to sort through massive amounts of literature.

Therefore, I cannot stress enough the importance of coming to the task with a positive attitude, because at first I thought sorting through the literature would be awful. But if I had kept that attitude then those 4 hours would have been the worse in my life, and not some of the easiest.

In all honesty, when it comes to psychology

placements, attitude is truly everything.

The New Term

After the Christmas break and I had sent off the updated spreadsheet for the Serious Games Literature Review, I was sent back to the mHealth review, because the PhD student who mainly supervises me, sent to the review to the official placement supervisor (who's a lecturer) and they both had some improvements for me to do.

Additionally, as the improvements were awhile ago, I don't really remember them. But in all honesty, I think there is somewhere important I can personally learn about academic writing from this term.

In academic writing, it really does need to be perfect and you do need to try to improve it as much as you can.

However, my argument always is, I personally feel like the university wants that from us, but they never give us any opportunities to learn how to do that.

For example, I have learnt so much about academic writing and how to be better at it this year, compared to any of the academic writing workshops or resources the university has ever provided me.

As well as I just think that is ridiculous in all fairness, because no one is ever born to be great at academic writing, no professor or lecturer was born that way, but then the university just expects us to be perfect academic writers when we go to university in first year.

Is that fair?

Of course not, but that isn't why I'm commenting on that specifically. I want to remind any readers here that if they are struggling with academic writing, you aren't alone, and if you're great at academic writing, then maybe please offer to help your fellow students out.

Just a thought (and that was basically the Over to You Section).

Overall, I am enjoying this placement because sure I might not be the busiest of placement students in the world, because I get work done to a high quality rather quickly (and my placement supervisor and PhD student have their own workloads to attend to). But I am learning.

And that is something that I have to keep reminding myself, my friends and my family when they question why I'm not down at university like all the other placement students (as far as I know there aren't any others but still), I have to stress that the entire point of my placement year is to learn.

You don't have to be in a physical location with the supervisor to learn, because as long as you are showing an interest, doing the work and trying to make the most of it. You are and will continue to learn, and that's what's important.

<u>Today's Meeting:</u>

Additionally, one of the entire points of me wanting to do a reflection today was my meeting, so I started the reflection before and I'm finishing it after, because there were a few useful points I wanted to make about it.

Therefore, it was me, my PhD student supervisor and my real supervisor on Skype and there was the normal conversations about how am I, how am I finding everything and those sorts of normal things.

But as I was writing that paragraph, I realised that was something important because I really want to stress to you that your placement provider (whoever it is) does care about you and making sure you're okay.

The vast, vast, vast majority of all placement providers are wonderful people who want to help, support and grow you as a person on your placement, so in case you are worried at all about being supported, please don't be.

Relax and remember to enjoy your placement.

(In all fairness, it will properly be the easiest year at university you'll have!)

So after the (important) normal topics were covered, my two supervisors started to talk about the mHealth review as we're starting to enter the final stages of the project, and they were thinking about what journals to pitch to.

Now this is brilliant in terms of placements, because you get to learn things you never ever would have considered beforehand. As I learnt how the whole academic publishing process worked, I already had a good idea because the publishing process is similar to the one us fiction writers use.

However, for academic papers, you have to research all the different journals that are related to your paper by using a database.

In case you ever need it, here's the link that we used.

- https://www.scimagojr.com/

Following that you need to find journals with good scores and basically you need to find journals that will be impressive to publish in.

A Massive Tip:

As you're been reading this helpful guide, I hope you know by now that I am not scared of making myself look like a fool, so here's another example of that.

So there we all were looking the internet for academic journals to possibly submit our paper to, but because the original conversations my two supervisors had weren't aimed at me, I didn't listen to it properly (and I'm fairly sure my internet turned down the volume on my main supervisor so I couldn't hear him perfectly).

The problem was when they were talking, my main supervisor explained how to find good journal to pitch, so there we were trying to find good journals.

But I didn't know what to do!

Now of course, normal people would ask questions, but I didn't for some reason, and it was only when one of them asked another question and I listened to the answer. Then I understood how to find good journals (that website link above is great!).

Moral of the story?

Please don't be afraid to ask questions, you are on your placement year to learn so do. Ask questions and your placement people will be great with you, so there is truly no harm done if you ask any a "silly" question.

And at the end of the day, we all asked silly questions before we became experts.

Rest of The Meeting

Following that eventful journal search, the rest of the meeting was about what I should do next in regards to the new literature review and the rest of the mHealth review.

My first job which will be extremely simple (I think and hope and pray) is to find more journals to submit our mHealth review too and create a list of priority journals for us.

This doesn't sound like a great task and it sounds like grunt work (because it is), but this is still a useful skill, because if you do want to work in Academica or move onto graduate programmes, then knowing how to find good journals is a great skill to have.

Also when you do your own experiments, literature reviews and research, it is critical that you use good sources of information.

Therefore, if you come across a great article but you aren't sure about the place where it was published, are you going to risk the snobby academic markers marking you down for using "bad" sources?

No.

It is probably a good idea to go on https://www.scimagojr.com/ and research the journal to see if it is any good or respectable.

Subsequently, my second job (and my three, fourth and fifth) is to go through the spreadsheet with all the relevant papers for our Serious Game Literature Review and go deeper.

This time round I will need to investigate the papers to see:

- If they used a game or toy
- If they were played with alone, with peers, family, etc.
- What problems were there with the papers.

And I'll tell you now, some of these papers are ridiculous, like some of them only had 4 participants. I'm sorry that would have no statistical power, and how the hell are you meant to draw conclusions about the entire autistic community based on four children?

So I think that will be a lot of fun (I want to say) because I do enjoy diving into papers and ripping them apart. Probably because it makes me feel like I actually know stuff before my academic writing lets me down!

<u>Over To You: Wrap Up</u>

At the end of this slightly larger than normal chapter, I wanted to remind you again the importance of coming at tasks in your placement with an open minded and a playful attitude, even when it is hard.

Because it would be so easy for me to be negative about having to go through those papers and do all that grunt work, but I'm not.

Since if I have a bad attitude going into tasks then I know I'll hate it, hate my placement and just hate this major part of my current life. I don't want that, and I really, really don't want you to feel like that during your placement.

So please, try to enjoy it and see even the grunt tasks as an opportunity to learn, and sometimes you'll be surprised at what you'll find.

A WEEK INTO EXAMINING PAPERS

As I write this reflection, I have been looking through the 1100 academic papers on the gamification of autism as part of the literature review I'll be writing up.

Now after doing this for a week, I want to explain the process a bit more and offer up a lot of useful tips and tricks to help you if you ever need to do such a thing. Because I promise you, this isn't as scary as it seems.

Therefore, for the past week I have been spending two hours a day looking through the spreadsheet and filling in the various columns and finding more general trends in the literature.

For example, for each paper I need to find out how many participants there are, was there a control group, a longitudinal study, if it was a game or not and other notes that might be useful.

Personally, I really do prefer this method and I'm

grateful for how my placement supervisor has laid it out because it allows me to be much more methodological in my analysis of the papers. Meaning I don't actually need to struggle to figure out what is important to note down.

However, I will add and this does apply to you that this is actually a lot easier than it seems. Since the abstract is your best friend here because a good one includes all the information you actually need. Then if you need to dive into the paper a bit more you can look at it later or right now.

And in case you actually think, you must look at all 1,100 papers in great depth. My question to you is simple, do you have nothing else to do in your life?

Because if it takes me a half an hour to look at ten papers in reasonable amounts of depth, it would took me over 550 hours to do the same for all the papers.

I don't have that time.

And to be honest, you will not use all 1,100 papers in the literature review anyway.

Sure you will use some and a fair amount of what I call "cornerstone" pieces. Like other literature reviews and you use their references to get started, and papers that you want to use to make a point. But you won't use anything close to 1,100 papers.

Also another handy trick for you to take advantage of is as all these papers are in a spreadsheet. I write SEE NOTES in one of the boxes in that row so when I come to writing my review I can use the find function, find the paper I wanted with the SEE NOTES part on it. Then I know exactly where that paper is.

As well as I only write SEE NOTES for papers that I want to use specifically to have a special point.

For example, so far there are about 3 papers that I want to reference because they accidently call into question the need for specially designed games for autistic children. Therefore, in my review that would be a great point to raise so I need to make sure I can quickly and easily find these papers.

Furthermore, the real point of going through these papers is to see the state of the literature and find the general trends. That's the real reason why you spend this time doing the looking, so you know the good and the bad about the literature.

As well as after the first few hundred papers, the major trends are clear as day and unless you're a really dedicated student (I applaud the people that are) then you start to laugh and your mind starts to wonder about how to make things more interesting.

For instance, I do not drink whatsoever but if I did then I would turn this into a drinking game. With the game being whenever I came across a paper with less than 10 participants I would take a shot.

Additionally, I make this point because that is how bad the research is in this area. The normal amount of participants is less than ten and that is simply outrageous.

How the hell are we meant to draw conclusions

about the entire autistic population from studies with such tiny amounts of participants?

You cannot.

Also I really admire some of the ambition from the researchers because so many of the papers want to make really grand conclusions and make such massive dents in the literature that they are willing to call their work ground-breaking.

Then they only have twenty participants, no control group and no longitudinal studies.

Even though this is rather funny to do because it is honestly laughable that journals actually allow these sorts of studies to get published. I am enjoying it because it is interesting and I am learning new things.

But you do start to get sarcastic in the comment section after a while. Now I would not encourage you to do this, but I am. Mainly because I know my sarcastic comments are hundreds of papers into the spreadsheet and my placement supervisor will not look that far down.

Yet I do have an awful habit of making comments on the amount of preliminary, pilot or incomplete studies in the literature. I mean finish your studies and then get them published, or just wait. (And no, not all of them are preregistrations)

So interesting times.

Conclusion:

Overall, the entire point of doing this reflection was to show you that you can easily breakdown what look like massive jobs into easy to manage chunks and develop ways of dealing with them.

That is what I cannot recommend enough, you need to develop your own ways of doing things that will help you get through this. As it did take me about a hundred papers to find a tips and tricks that helped me enjoy this massive task.

Let's face it, looking through 1,100 papers doesn't look easy at first!

So please whether you are on your placement now or in the future, remember to find ways that work for you and try and enjoy the massive tasks. Sometimes once you get into them and find a rhythm that works for you, they can actually be rather interesting.

And remember to use more than 10 participants in your own ground-breaking studies!

AFTER THE BEHEMOTH TASK

After two and a bit weeks, I have finally finished going through all those pages, and there are a few things I want to reflect on and share with you. As well as the points I'll be sharing will help you to become better researchers and they may help you find weaknesses for the critical analysis sections of your assignments.

Things To Reflect On:

At some point during your placement in the future or now, you will be faced with a massive task that looks overwhelming. That is exactly what going through these papers seemed a first.

I really didn't want to look through all of these papers and everything seemed to be going okay for the first few hundred. Then I got to paper 400 out of 1200 and I was just... seriously? I have to do another 600.

Now I fully imagine if the task was something

else and not a literature review filled with repetitive (and awful) studies. Then I am sure this wouldn't have been so dull come paper 400, but as you'll see later on, all these papers had basically the same faults and same results.

So I had to power through, and I'll explain some tips in a moment about how you can reframe a problem like this.

However, I would like to return to a great benefit of placements from earlier in the book. Placements allow you to test the water in the psychology job market.

Now I absolutely know without a shadow of a doubt that I will not become a psychology researcher in my psychology career. That just does not interest me in the slightest, but before my placement I didn't know that.

In addition, before this placement I had no idea how to do a proper literature review, because like everything what secondary (high) school teaches us is often very different to university level work.

For instance, a literature review back in secondary school was find 15 papers, write what they found and what was good and bad about each one.

To be honest it isn't that far off a university-level literature review. Except for the fact that you need to do it with thousands of papers and you talk more generally about the papers and the literature as a whole.

Hence the name: literature review.

Therefore, this placement has allowed me to get a deeper understanding of how literature reviews are researched, written up and published.

All critical things if I wanted a job in psychology research.

<u>Finding Your Rhythm</u>

This is one of the tricks whenever you come across a massive task on your placement. You need to find your rhythm, even if you have to cheat slightly.

And what I mean my that is when looking through these papers, I was meant to find the full paper, read the entire thing then fill out the columns on the spreadsheet.

Such as:

- Did it have a control group?
- Was it a longitudal study?
- What social interaction did it have?
- How many participants?
- Who appeared in the study?

And on and on and on!

Therefore, I am not ashamed to say I did not do that in the slightest. My life is far too short because I could still get great results for what was needed using a different method.

So what did I do?

I focused on the abstracts. Since a good abstract tells you everything you need to know including the participant numbers and factors, and the results. This all allowed me to get a great amount of information for all the different papers.

As well as here's another little secret of the trade. The spreadsheet I was using was compiled using different searches on different academic databases. Meaning there were duplicate entries, so I managed to delete about 200 papers.

I was more than happy with that!

<u>What I Am Not Saying:</u>

Of course I am not encouraging you to cheat or do less work during your placement.

What I am saying is sometimes you don't need to work harder, but smarter.

<u>Mind Tricks To Reframe The Task</u>

Then I cannot recommend enough when you're doing a massive task, is to reframe it somehow and make yourself laugh when you're doing it.

For example, after seeing 400 different papers with less than 10 participants. I was growing so bored of seeing that stupid amount of participants so I joked with myself that if I drank. I should create a drinking game when I would take a shot for each study I saw that had under 10 participants.

No joke, if you did that drinking game with the Gamification of Autism literature, you would pass out after looking at ten studies. That's how bad the participant numbers are.

I do not drink alcohol (no, it isn't for religious reasons). But it made myself laugh, smile and it gave me a bit of energy to continue and keep seeing all these studies with less than 10 participants.

Things To Share:

As a result of looking at these papers, I want to mention three things that can help you design better research in the future.

Firstly, please use an appropriate number of participants in your sample size. Ten participants in a study that is meant to represent an entire population is not good enough.

It is honestly laughable.

It is like me saying all the men in my family represent all the men in the world. That isn't truth and that is laughable.

So please, use statistics to calculate the number of participants that you need for your study to have statistical power.

In addition, as a whole, the autism literature is very skewed towards males. Even the diagnosis is mainly aimed at males with females being underrepresented in the literature.

Therefore, when it comes to your own studies, make sure you look into what you're researching to make sure you avoid or perhaps even remedy any gender biases in the literature of your area.

Secondly, a quick note on technology in research. I encourage you to research the effects of technology on human behaviour, but make sure you are aware of the temporal validity. Especially since technology changes and advances all the time. Even more so with the advent of the Metaverse and Web 3.0 in the coming years.

As a result, when it comes to you designing your study, it is a good idea to look for ways to increase the validity of your results even as technology changes.

Finally, please, please, please use a control group and longitudinal study if you can. Of course, I know the longitudinal research is more difficult so let's forget that part.

However, control groups are critical in research as they allow you to see if your experiment is actually having an effect on your participants. So that is definitely something to bear in mind for the future.

Due to at the end of the day, we all want our research to be as good as possible so our results can make an meaningful impact in the literature.

And you never know, you might get slightly famous for your results, but that's impossible if you do half-assed research.

Or at the very least, let's all do the best research we can so you can all pass our degrees!

THE UNIVERSITY LOOKS AFTER YOU AND BACK TO UNIVERSITY DAYS

I just came back from a Back To University day at my university for placement students to meet with university staff, talk about their experience and recap on important topics needed for our coursework.

However, before I start talking about that and why they are extremely useful for us as placement students. I want to remind you of a great example of how the university looks after you.

Since at my university, we need to hand in Placement Evaluation Forms during Week 10, 20 and 30 (or whenever the placement finishes) of the academic year, as well as our placement supervisor submits one too.

The official and main reason why the university gets you to do this is because they want to see how the placement supervisors sees you're getting on.

Then this forms part of your overall mark for your placement year.

However, a secondary reason for this is so the university can read your evaluation and see how you're getting on. To see if you're okay, enjoying it and are actually doing activities that will benefit your future psychology career.

Personally, this is great from my perspective because I knew if there was a problem. Then there is a chance for the university to be told and they can sort it out.

Why Back To University Days Are Important?

Moving onto the main point of this chapter, I now want to explain what are Back To University days.

The official (and rather boring) explanation is they are a chance for you to check in with the university and see other students. And considering our first one of these was cancelled due to Strikes. I didn't think too much more of these days.

But now I have attended one, I really want to stress they're great, and these are not something you should just ignore.

For example (and we will be serious in a moment), most universities offer you free tea, coffee and lunch. Personally that is a great reason to go. I always, always love a freebie and especially if it's free good quality coffee.

Yes, I am extremely easy that way.

In addition, it is actually rather great to see, talk

and hear about other people's experience. Since in my placement I don't get to mix with a massive range of people with it just being me, my Placement Supervisor and his PhD student.

Therefore, it was great to go to the Back to University Day (B2UD) and see other people.

Also they all tended to have some great stories from their placements. Which I'll talk about in a moment and in the next chapter so you can hear about their experiences.

Equally, you'll find these days to be very validating. Since (I will not be sending this to my university) one of the great things about research placements is they tend to be on the… lighter side of placements.

Due to as long as the work gets done and I've tried my best, my supervisor couldn't care less about how long I spent on it.

Personally, I felt rather bad because I was pretending that I was working six hours a day on the work. But in reality, it was more like two or three.

However, I was talking to one of my friends-of-a-friend who was also doing a research placement and we were laughing over the fact that we both did the exact same.

So the point of this little section is B2UD are great for seeing people and knowing if what you're doing is right, wrong or how to improve.

Then later in the chapter and in the next one, I'll explain some of their own experiences so you can get some broader opinions rather than only my own.

Structure Of The Day

As much as I make it sound like one big social, I have to mention that there was an actual structure for the day that was helpful in some regards, and not in others.

The first session was an introduction where we all talked, mentioned what was the best and hardest thing about our placements (next chapter) and the Lecturer who was leading the day introduced some things.

The fact that I cannot remember that just speaks to how important they were.

Afterwards, there was a statistics refresher. Now this was great in theory because as we move onto the writing up of our research projects, we'll have to conduct our data analysis and do some statistics.

That was fine, and this was one of the reasons why this day was so useful.

The problem. The problem was because the Teaching Assistant couldn't make it to teach the recap live, it was a replay of last year's Statistics Refresher that was done on teams.

Again no problem there.

But it was an hour long.

Now I do not want you to judge me for not being able to concentrate for an entire hour watching a statistics video, but I'm sorry. An hour is too long for something like that.

And after the video I spoke to other people and

we all managed to pay attention for the first twenty minutes (lots of people didn't stay that long to be fair) then none of us were interested.

Nonetheless, I really have to congratulate the woman who was leading the B2UD, because she really tried. She really, really tried to make the statistic refresher interesting, but I think even she gave up in the end.

Thankfully, the slides for the Statistic Refresher video are online so if needed, we can all look at them again later.

The lesson for this section is, please don't worry about the statistics part of your coursework too much before this event. The university knows you haven't done statistics in over a year, so they'll help you out.

But whilst we're talking about statistics, I'm sure this will date the book slightly. Yet it seemed like the university did a change over to their statistic programmes during the pandemic, since I was taught SPSS during my first in-person year.

Now the university is teaching students R. Which is meant to be a great free piece of statistical software that is becoming the dominate force in psychology and it is what companies are looking for.

I'm sure by the time this book comes out, R will well and truly be the norm in psychology. But I wanted to write these few paragraphs so any young people in a few years time can find out how us dinosaurs used to conduct Statistics.

Ha!

The Only Bad Experience I heard:

Before I finish up this chapter, I want to tell you about the only bad placement experience I heard all day, and please know I did talk to a lot of people. Therefore, when I say the vast, vast majority of placement students were having great times at their placements. It's the truth.

However, there was this woman on our table and I swear I knew her from somewhere other than my psychology lectures.

Anyway, she worked at her former college and she was helping out in the Mental Health and Wellbeing department. That sounds great and she was really looking forward to it, and she likes it how everyone there is really nice to her.

Then the problems started to appear.

She wasn't allowed to do anything. She wasn't allowed to sit in with teachers talking to students. The students weren't allowed to talk to her, but they did, and that really (and I mean REALLY) annoyed the staff.

So instead of doing psychology related things on her placement, she only did three things because she wasn't allowed to do anything else. She checked students out of the school, she printed out labels and she played puzzles on the computer.

She was not allowed to do anything else.

Period.

Subsequently, she did refer the issue to the university and the placement people did have a talk with her college. Nothing happened and this is partly because the placement department is made up of three women.

That is it.

It is sadly so small so they were busy, and all three are amazing people, but their time is limited. As well as I'm sure the Director of Placements mentioned she was a researcher too.

Yet the Placement Department is trying to help her.

I really hope she gets things sorted, so she can actually get some experience.

<u>Warning On Last Section!</u>

The only reason for this warning section is because that is the only bad experience I heard all day, and I don't want you to think all placements are bad because of that one example.

As well as, as we are all psychology people here, I want to remind you of the Peak-End Rule, one of the thinking biases. Which (in short) proposes people tend to remember the most interesting point of an event and the end of it. Then they don't remember the things in-between

Please don't remember placements being bad and forget all the positive things I've mentioned in this book.

Just wanted to make you aware of that as we move forward into a very exciting section, because I get to reflect on what other people have said about their placements.

And you get to hear about other experiences besides mine.

PLACEMENT EXPEREINCES FROM OTHER PEOPLE AND EXTREMELY USEFUL TIPS

As we continue with our look at what happened at my Back To University Day in this chapter I wanted to explore what other people told me about their placements. Since unlike me, lots of people had hospitals, wellbeing and other types of placements.

As well as whilst I won't specifically look at each type of placement, there are a number of general themes that I didn't experience in my own placement, so I'll tell you about them now.

<u>What Did Students Find Good About Their Placements?</u>

Therefore, lots of people found their placements good because it gave them real life experiences in that sector of the psychology job market.

For example, I was talking to two people who

worked in a local hospital Trust and they were pleased to experience what that was like. In terms of talking to patients, referring them and helping people make sense of their so-called problems.

Now I say so-called, because anyone who does clinical psychology should know that mental health "problems" are maladaptive coping mechanisms to help the person cope with everyday life. Therefore, the actually coping mechanisms need to change so they are helpful, but it is the causes of the psychological distress is the problem. Not the person.

Anyway, lots of students enjoyed having that sort of real world experience, and the two I was talking to said the past few months so great that they wanted to work in the hospital in the future.

Personally, I love hearing about the experiences of others, because it was interesting to hear about their perspectives and what working in a non-research placement was like. As well as it was really interesting to hear all the bureaucracy and protection guidelines they have to follow.

As a person who used to work with children as a volunteer and I'm currently a student Ambassador with my university, I had some idea about the protection measures since I have an Enhanced DBS check amongst other protective measurements. But as you're working with people's medical records, there are even more measures to protect the patients.

Additionally, other placements students liked the people. This happened in two different areas. The people they worked with and the people they interacted with as part of their job.

In terms of hospital settings, other students really enjoyed getting to know and work alongside psychologists and medical doctors as these were the experts, and some had really interesting conversations with them.

Personally, that is the reason why placements are great. It is these people that you mine for information and learning from that makes it all worthwhile.

Especially, as I say in my books and on my podcast that university and textbooks teach us the theory and how to apply it. But it is the real-world and professional people that teach us how to really use it in the world.

Then in other placements, like in Colleges, schools and my own research settings, other students were surprised at how useful and positive the people they worked with were.

Additionally, if I too draw on my own experience. I am not exactly the most social of people at first glance, and I don't like mixing with too many people (one of the few downsides of Autism), so I was nervous about my placement.

But I have to admit it was great to meet my placement supervisor and his PhD student. They were great people, supportive and very helpful, and even though I am not working down at the university with them (I'm pretty sure the PhD student isn't either), I still feel like part of the team.

Finally, the last major thing students found good about their placement was the networking. Technically this isn't too different to the last positive thing, but there is more of a focus here. As this applies to everything about interacting with supervisors, staff and patients.

Networking refers to building up a list of contacts that you can keep in contact with and return to in the future.

And this is why the chapter refers to extremely useful tips, because you HAVE to use this placement opportunity to network. That will be golden for you in the future, and if you think placements are only for learning new skills. You have clearly forgotten networking.

Since if you work in a hospital under a psychologist and it turns out you really like working there. Then make sure you're on good terms with the psychologist when you leave, and make sure you're on friendly terms with other people too and they know how useful you are.

Afterwards make sure you keep in contact with them and after you've finished your studies and have a Masters or PhD, contact them again and ask if there's any work.

As well as since they know how useful you are and how great you were during your placement, they'll probably jump at the chance to have you back. Since you already have a rough idea how the department works (you might need a refresher but still), you know the sort of patients they deal with and you know how the other staff members work.

It's basic networking.

And this really was a recurring theme of the day, lots of different people were talking about the benefits of the people they met and they were now part of their network.

For example, the friend-of-a-friend I was talking to was doing a different research placement to me and he's been attending a lot of university talks and seminars. Allowing him to talk and network with a wide range of people, he never would have met without the placement.

This is another reason why I write books and podcast because I have met so many amazing people through this, including you.

So all in all networking is very powerful and a placement provides you with the perfect opportunity.

What Some People Found Hard?

Now we need to talk about what people found hard about their placements, because truth be told, if I say I was the only one having occasional problems with the placement. You would think I'm a liar, and I am far from that.

Therefore, the first problem people are having with the placement was the commute. Personally, I was no exception and that's why I have never complained about my placement being remote. Otherwise, my commute would be two and quarter hours just to get there.

Not my idea of fun!

Thankfully, this isn't a problem anymore because I passed my driving test last month so I can drive thankfully. But the cost of petrol is slightly making that a problem, and I think at something I'll have to decide what's more important. My time or my money (The train's a lot cheaper!).

Anyway, the commute can be concerning to students and the only tips I can offer would be:

- Attempt to choose a placement you can easily get to.
- Perhaps try to live closer to your placement.
- Try a remote placement if needed?

All those options have their own positives and negatives, but the commute can be a tough pill to swallow.

Secondly, lots of students are having problems with their research projects. I am sort of amongst them since I am doing a literature review as this part of my coursework and I'm hoping they'll except it. But I am not sure if this is allowed.

(At least I'm still doing a lot of research work so they cannot say I'm not learning or doing any research tasks)

Anyway, other students were having difficulties with the write-up, and understanding what exactly they needed to do. Which I forget to say was what we covered in the afternoon of the Back to University Day, so the woman leading the Day explained everything to us, and that was really helpful.

Therefore, that negative point is sort of made redundant, as the afternoon was spend fixing that issue.

NHS Research Rules

Before I move onto the last main theme of what people found hard, I wanted to talk about the NHS research rules so UK students can understand the problems so they don't get a nasty shock when they start their placements. Or if you're on your placement now, you might want to have a look immediately.

For international readers, the NHS is our National Health Service which provides UK citizens with free health care.

Consequently, the NHS has very strict rules about research because they handle patient data and these rules are very… they are just awful. For instance, students were telling us that the NHS doesn't allow you to call it research and if you're making generalisations, that's a no-no. Instead you need to frame it in a certain way and there are so many little rules like that.

Of course I am NOT saying don't do your placements in the NHS. Since it can/will provide you with some amazing experiences that can really help you in the future and dramatically increase your employability.

But just be aware that you might need to start sorting out your research project before other people in your cohort do. Just to make sure you get through all the NHS red tape and still have enough time to conduct your "research".

(I think it's funny you're not allowed to do "research".)

Harsh Realities

If you're read any of my books, reflective books or listened to my podcast. Then you know that from time to time, I talk about the realities of being a clinical psychologist and working in the real world based on what my friends and other professionals have said.

But it is one thing to know about it, and another thing to see it.

Since if I say to you that not everything who needs psychological help gets it and even goes for treatment, not everyone wants to believe they have a mental health condition amongst other things.

Then you're probably going to be a bit sad for the person because we know as psychology students that psychological treatment is amazing, and can really improve lives.

All psychology students at least understand that even at a surface level. Even if you don't understand the reasons why, you understand that basic idea.

However, if you're working in a hospital and you see that a person who is kind, helpful and a great person clearly has a mental health condition, and needs therapy. But that person refuses treatment, then that will be hard.

It will be hard because as psychology people, we

want to help others. As I mention in my *Clinical Psychology Reflections Volume 1*, it is the unofficial mandate of psychologists to help people, decrease psychological distress and improve lives.

So it hurts a lot when people don't allow themselves to be helped, and they stop us from completing our mandate.

Of course, then the students say how the placement has helped them to develop a thicker skin and helped them to be more professional.

So that is something you need to bear in mind, prepare yourself for and develop a thick skin. Because you sadly cannot help everyone.

Also just because I can feel myself starting to be effected by the bias, remember the first 80% of this chapter was extremely positive that includes the other two minor negatives. Remember the peak-end rule and make sure this talk about harsh realities doesn't obscure your view about how great placements are in general.

Because I can promise you, they are great!

THE NEW LITERATURE REVIEW
Wow!

I am seriously bad at making sure I do these reflections in a timely manner since I started this new literature a month ago as I write this, and I have a lot to tell you about, reflect on and give tips.

With the first tip being, as I've mentioned before, please make sure you stay on top of your reflective coursework.

<u>Meeting and You Aren't The Centre of The World:</u>

One of the reasons why I was so behind in these reflections is simply because after I sorted out the massive literature review table and went through the research. I sent it off but then some things were going on at the university that meant my placement supervisor had to focus on them and not me for a few weeks.

In the grand scheme of things, this equally did and did not matter. It didn't matter because in other placement settings, like a hospital, this wouldn't happen to often simply because all placement supervisors do focus on you.

However, the very nice thing that I've learnt about research placements, at least at my university, is the amount of freedom and flexibility they offer you. Since I mentioned in the last reflection how as long as you get your work done in a timely manner, they don't actually care. Which is very true in my case, because I do the work quickly and effectively they tend to be more relaxed about leaving me to my own devices.

All in all, it will be rare for you to be left without instructions for a while, but you aren't the centre of your placement supervisor's universe.

Especially, in the world of academia since your placement supervisor will be teaching, do final year project supervisions, having to deal with strikes and more!

Therefore, please, if you're in this type of situation of course email them and ask what's going on but please cut them some slack. Academia is not a good working environment, so it is best to give your supervisors some leeway.

Anyway, so it got to the three week point and the next day I was going up to London for two days for a major international conference when I get an email requesting a meeting with me, my placement supervisor and his PhD student.

Thankfully I had been wanting a meeting and to move on with the literature review, and I was coming home each night of the conference anyway. So I agreed to the meeting and it happened.

Well!

As a student there are times when you realise how much of a student you really are. This was one of those times. Due to my supervisor and his PhD student were talking away about professional literature reviews, and it dawned on me how little I knew about graphs, literature tables and other things that professional ones do to APA standards.

In fact before all this I had no clue about how to create graphs to APA standards.

Overall, the meeting was completed, I was given the green light to start writing the literature review and I have plenty of tips to give you about writing your own literature reviews.

Literature Review Tips:

It turns out a fair amount of professional reviews use what are known as summary tables where they summarise all the research within a specific time period or other measure. And these are used to help make it easier for the reader to understand the gist of the research that was done. Therefore, in our literature review we're going to do a table for the past five years probably.

I'll mention in a future chapter about how to do that, but I'm telling you this so you're aware of it. Since doing a summary table is a very professional thing to do and that might give you a few extra marks.

Additionally, including charts and graphs is another very beneficial feature to add to your literature reviews (and reports too) since it is a good visual way to relay information to the reader, and it helps to convey your point across.

For example, we did graphs for the following points:

- Pie Chart showing the diversity of tasks used.
- Pie chart showing within versus between subject design studies.
- Histogram of the age distributing of participants.

Granted that turned into a bar chat very quickly because Excel wasn't playing ball with me!

- Histogram showing the distribution of the sample sizes.
- Pie Chart showing control vs no control group in the literature.

As a result, even though these charts and graphs don't sound too exciting, they can actually be very powerful in your literature review. They can easily and reliably relay information to your reader and they can make certain topics so much easier to write about.

For instance, if we take the pie chart about within versus between subject design. At first thought I had no clue what to write about that point, but because I created the chart and found only 10% (if that) of gamification studies used within subject designs. It gave me a starting point and that made writing up that paragraph or two a lot easier.

And as students, don't we want everything to be a bit easier?

Excel Tip:

Whilst I fully admit I haven't looked at the APA formatting for graphs and charts yet (and yes I really know I should have), I decided to create my charts and graphs in Microsoft excel then my plan is format them properly at the end of the my first draft.

However, as much as I love Excel, there is a massive problem when it comes to formatting groups. Since if you put anything that looks like a date in the cells, it will automatically convert that to a date.

Such as I wanted to create a group for a bar chart that had *1-10* participants, but Excel converted that into *01-Oct*. Not what I wanted!

Thankfully I managed to find out how to fix this, and in case you ever need this tip I'm sharing it with you now. Therefore, to format the cell correctly I would start off by putting a 0 into it. Then press control + 1 and that will allow you to format it.

After the formatting tab opens, you need to go to Number> Custom and then type in what you want your category to be.

I know it sounds complex but once you do that, it will start to make sense.

I really hope that doesn't take you as long to work out and fix as it did for me!

Conclusion:

In the next chapter, I'll start to actually reflect on my experience of writing up the literature review and I'll probably remember some other tips to give you. But this is why I like placements, they give you a great opportunity to learn about certain things that you don't learn in the lecture theatre and you get to develop your skills in ways that most students can't.

HOW DID I FIND WRITING A LITERATURE REVIEW FROM SCRATCH?

I should probably start off this chapter with a little clarification because I didn't really start writing the literature review from scratch, but that is still an accurate title for the chapter because of two main reasons.

Firstly, during the meeting about writing this review, me, my supervisor and his PhD student created a write-up plan that detailed out things like what charts and graphs to create, the sort of guidelines I would create for the future directions of the literature and something about designing tables which I must clarify.

However, as you and me know, a plan is all well and good but when it comes to academic writing. A plan really only goes so far because the plan didn't cover anything about what to include in the introduction, the main body and direction of the review and so on.

Therefore, I basically did do this review from complete scratch because it really is only now I'm writing up with reflection that the write-up plan was useless.

Well… not exactly but more on that later.

Secondly, my experience of writing up literature reviews is very slight for starters, because the mHealth review is the only other professional one I've done. As well as a good third of that review was completed before it got handed over to me and even then there were still plenty of notes and section headings to work with.

But please, as you'll probably remember from the beginning of the book, the person I took over from was a wonderful person, just not that good at referencing, translating what was in her brain onto paper so I could follow it, and I'm fairly sure that I did basically rewrite that entire review.

Overall, on second thought, I basically did write this from scratch, but I suppose that this is another great example of self-doubt. I doubted how much work I had put into this review, so definitely remember when you are (or currently) on your placement to make sure not to doubt yourself!

How Am I Finding It?

When people say that starting is the hardest thing to do, they aren't lying. Due to I had done all the research and I knew the literature very well, but I had no clue whatsoever about how to take what I learnt in those 1000+ papers and convert it down into an introduction to start off with.

That was hard.

Therefore, I flicked through my mHealth review and another literature review that my supervisor and his PhD student had done earlier in 2021. I started to look at the structure and what was included and thankfully I managed to start.

Introduction Reflection

Once I got going by introducing serious games then autism and the need for the literature review. I definitely found it a lot easier as then I moved onto a general overview of the literature as that's what my supervisors did in their one.

And there's a tip for you on your placement. You need to remember that whatever work you do, you aren't alone. You can (and need to) ask for help, look at other reviews and remember that in this information age it is easy to find resources to help you.

So make use of them!

In addition, another tip I would give you is when I got to the end of the introduction, I didn't know the direction of the literature review was going. If you already know the direction then that is perfect and definitely better, but sometimes you don't.

Therefore, in the final paragraph where you include a sentence along the lines of *"This review will examine… by investigating the following…"* what I did here was I left it blank and once I wrote the conclusion I went back and filled it in.

Personally I really think that was helpful for me because it meant I didn't need to worry about being restricted by what I put in the introduction from the start. And yes you can always change things but I really didn't want to have to keep going back to the introduction every five minutes to update it, more or less.

Main Body Reflection

In terms of the main body, it was another difficult section to start off with because the biggest problem with the gamification literature is how bad it is. Meaning there are very little positive things you can review and reflect on, but I was determined to find something positive to mention.

Therefore, I focused on the promising results and the one or two methodological advantages.

Then I was hit with another problem, how do I take all the bad things about the literature (and believe me there are tons!) and condense it all down into something readable and doesn't go on for twenty thousand words?

Also another problem with all the bad in the literature is all the negatives are themes running throughout its entirety. So I couldn't simply pick out one or two studies and talk about them. I needed to talk about the entire literature and try to make empirical points about it.

That was hard.

Well thankfully that's where the write-up plan

came in because I was asked to make some graphs and charts to demonstrate different things about the literature. As a result, I focused on using those charts as the bones of my main body then my explanation of the chart and the negatives related to it were the muscles and rest of the body so to speak.

Wow that analogy just got weird!

Anyway once I worked out that the main body also got a lot easier to work on, and this is another tip for you in a way. If you ever come into a problem with something you're doing, make sure you take a step back and make sure you aren't overthinking it, and you don't already have a tool to help you.

I wish I had realised a few minutes sooner about using the charts as the bones of the main body.

Discussion Section

Moving onto the penultimate section, I will fully admit I did struggle with the discussion section because I still am. In fact I have said to my supervisor's PhD student, you can definitely tell it's a first draft and I do want guidance on improving it.

Then he unintentionally reminded me of another tip or two actually that I want to mention now. On your placement (and this is something I need to get better at) you need to cut yourself some slack. You will not be great at everything and you certainly will not be great or perfect at something you just started a few months ago.

Like I will not be great at writing literature reviews or academic writing for that matter in the space of a few months. Granted I am really improving because for the first time in my university "life" I have two great people who actually want to help me and they make suggestions on improvements. But I need to remember I will not be great at literature reviews for now, I will get better and I will continue to get better over time.

And that goes for you too. You need to remember you're trying, you're learning and you're doing the best you possibly can. That's enough and that's all anyone can ask of you.

To finish up the discussion section reflection, I will definitely be getting feedback on it and I will reflect on that when I get it so you and me know what to do in the future.

Future Direction, Conclusion and Abstract

Just to get rid of the conclusion and abstract reflections, I just styled them on the literature review that my placement supervisor and his student did together. Since that's a professional-level review and I want to learn that sort of professional structure for my own academic writing.

Furthermore, I think the future direction section was another one I slightly struggled with because it seemed a bit too short and slightly repetitive of what I mentioned in the main body, so my feedback on that section should be interesting.

Then again it might have been because what we decided to do with this future direction section was create guidelines for future research.

As well as if you're unfamiliar with "normal" future direction sections, you normally suggest the direction of the field of whatever you're looking at. For example, if you're looking at the genes behind depression. You might suggest researchers should stop looking at the 5-HTT gene and focus more on another one.

That is just a completely fictional example yet you get my point. It's about steering researchers instead of creating guidelines.

However, the field of gamification greatly needs guidelines to improve their research because it is such low quality. It is impossible to draw any sort of scientific conclusions from.

Therefore, it was generally a matter of rephrasing what I mentioned in the main body, so the feedback will definitely be interesting.

<u>Chapter's Conclusion:</u>

To wrap up this chapter, as much as this chapter has shown how difficult some sections were to write up. I must admit it was rather nice to do it, because I do "enjoy" or rather like doing all this writing up. Sure, I might not be great at it but I am learning, developing my skills and wanting to be better. And that's the entire point of a degree in the first place.

That's why I always try to recommend doing a placement year because without it, I certainly wouldn't be improving or have the skills I do now.

AFTER THE FIRST AND FINAL IMPROVEMENTS

After getting back and doing the improvements for my gamification literature review, I wanted to reflect on them and offer a few tips that might actually help you.

Thankfully, my gamification literature review was a lot better than the last one, because even though there are technically 55 comments on improvements. It turned out that most of them weren't actually major things or improvements per se.

Since some of the comments was when he decided to change something and he wanted to explain it to me.

Now that is something that I did want to highlight. And this is why I actually really like this placement year because your supervisors will (or should at least) take the time to "sit down" with you and explain how to improve. I learnt a lot by the improvements and changes that my supervisor's PhD student made.

Yet this was only possible because he took the time to explain them to me, and this is a very annoying thing about academics as a whole. Due to they are so overworked and pushed for time, they normally just mark your work without offering up any sort of feedback.

Thankfully placements are different.

In addition, I was pleasantly surprised at the amount of red in Track Changes on the literature review. Because in the mHealth review, partly because I inherited it from the last placement student and partly because of my own lack of professional academic writing, there wasn't a single line or paragraph that hasn't changed.

This time there were some rather large chunks of texts that weren't changed in the slightest.

As well as something else that was very pleasant about these improvements was we've all known academics that think themselves far superior to everyone else, even if they don't mean it.

Therefore, if you gave them a piece of work and they wanted to add something (I'm talking about a joint paper as my name, my supervisor and his PhD student's names are all on the paper because we all worked on it when it goes for publication). These stuck-up academics would make the change and not offer you a chance to have it explained or to get your thoughts on it.

These improvements weren't like that because in

this placement, it's team work, and that probably goes for all placements too. As well as because you and your peers on placement are a team, it is a great place to learn about how to improve.

Also something I will mention is YouTube is your friend.

I'm saying this because I think I mentioned it before in another reflection, but I sent off my first draft with tables and figures that I just knew were not to APA standard, and the PhD student was very good about it. Because he knew it was just something I didn't know how to do and he was going to teach it to me.

Therefore, I finished up the improvements and I thought I might as well watch some YouTube videos and do these tables and figures myself.

I was surprised at how great some of the videos were and APA 7th edition tables and figures aren't hard to do.

And this is what's critical about placements and learning as a whole on two fronts.

Firstly, you need to be a proactive learner in all areas of university life, and if you do that then it will really help you improve your education and learn new skills.

Secondly, all these skills like how to do tables, how to do professional literature reviews and how to do professional academic writing. These are all skills that will help you for years to come in your Final Year Project and whatever higher-higher education you might decide to go onto. Like a Master's or a PhD.

Therefore, I know I'll mention this again more broadly in the conclusion but you really can learn so much about improving your academic skills with an academic placement.

Also this goes for all placements. Regardless of what placement you pick and get on, you will learn more than you can possibly realise, and that's the real root of my surprise because I didn't know I had improved this much.

And to be honest, it really does give me a lot of hope for next year at university. Especially considering how relatively hopeless I was about academic writing in earlier chapters of this book.

Feelings About Endings

Before we move on to the conclusion, I do really want to quickly (that's always a relative term with me) mention endings, because your placements will end, and even if you don't think you will have a reaction to when the placement is up. You probably will.

Especially if it's been very positive.

Personally, I never ever thought I would feel something towards the ending of my placement. Sure I really enjoyed it, it suited my lifestyle perfectly and I got to meet great people.

But I wasn't sure if I was going to be "sad" (a bit of a strong term but you get the idea) about the placement ending. And the reason for this is probably because you've basically just spent the past academic year with great people, doing great projects and you're enjoyed your time with them.

So of course this is nothing to be ashamed or concerned about, it is a reminder that we are all human and everything ends at some point.

But on the flip side, at least I get to work with my placement supervisor again next year, go to his socials with the rest of his students and see people from his year as he's my Final Year Project supervisor. As well as then there's the social tonight so I get to see everyone.

However, now that the placement is over. Let's bring everything together and I can give you my final and full opinion of the past year, do I recommend placements and any final tips for both future and current placement students.

CONCLUSION: DO I RECOMMEND PLACEMENTS AND OTHER FINAL TIPS?

One of the most basic purposes of this entire book was for you to get an understanding of what a placement is like, the sort of things you'll be doing and most importantly was it interesting.

Therefore, after reading the past 17+ chapters, I think it's safe to say that we all have a much better understanding of what a placement is, or at the very least an academic placement.

However, that's something that I want to address first of all. Just because I did an academic placement doesn't mean that my core points aren't right for you too, regardless of the type of placement you choose.

Since on your placement, you will undoubtably get to network with some great people who actually want you to improve, succeed and enjoy your time with them.

Additionally, you'll get to learn tons of new things. I've already mentioned about research skills and academic writing skills. But if you work in a hospital for example, you would get to learn a lot more about the daily life of a psychotherapist and what they actually do. As well as all the challenges, delights and problems that aren't mentioned in the textbooks.

Will this always be positive?

Of course not, and I have mentioned some negatives throughout the book to, and my core point about this benefits you is definitely true in my experience. And out of everyone in my cohort who went on placement, only two or three had bad experiences out of 30+ people.

That's a very good rate.

Final Tips

Before I give you and explain my final verdict on psychology placements, I want to offer you some tips for both current and future placement students.

If you're reading this book and you're currently on placement. I cannot recommend enough that you dive into every opportunity given to you to deepen your learning and understanding. Some of those opportunities will be great and be extremely beneficial.

In addition, definitely go to the socials if that's something your placement does. I mentioned earlier in the book about my own fears about going to university socials but I'm so glad that I did. And I am really looking forward to the social tonight.

It's basically very fun networking, something that could be extremely useful to you.

Finally, and this is to both sets of students,

remember to have fun. Having a placement year isn't about having a full-time job or a grind, it's about having fun and enjoying that year of your life.

Therefore, make sure you pick a placement that you will find fun in the first place. As well as if you're currently on placement make sure you try to enjoy it as much as you can or find ways to do that.

Life is way too short not to have fun.

Then because that was a joint tip, for future placement students. If you really want a placement, definitely apply for as many as you can because that was probably a mistake that I made.

A mistake that worked out perfectly but if my university lecturer didn't accept me then I was screwed.

Please don't get into the same boat as I could have.

Lastly, try to use your placement as a tester for a future career or maybe pick a placement with purpose. For example, if you want to be a psychotherapist, then pick a placement working with a psychotherapist so you can test out if you enjoy that sort of career.

Try out different options because it's better you start to have an idea about what you want to do now, compared to going to a day job in a few years time, finding out you hate it and effectively being stuck there for a while, or maybe forever.

Just some ideas.

The Question Of The Book

Therefore, I suppose this book all comes down to my next question: do I really recommend placements for students?

Yes.

I wholeheartedly do recommend you do a psychology placement if you can, and even though I was basically always going to say this because of the benefits I've had from this.

This opinion has only increased rather dramatically in the past week since I got my improvements back.

Due to when I started this placement I was had only scraped past the minimum requirements by 1%. Not because I didn't know the information or I was a bad psychology student, but because my academic writing wasn't good.

As well as whenever I tried to improve my academic writing and get help from the university. I struggled to get it and no one actually took the time to help me.

Of course I completely understand and know (even more after this year) how overworked, basically abused and mistreated academics are by the university in their working conditions. But it would be great if universities could improve themselves so academics would have a bit more time for helping students out too.

Therefore, I love placements because it is very one-on-one, the supervisors have time, effort and they actually want to sit down with you and help you.

They want you to improve and they want you to learn.

Personally I absolutely would have hated to go into my final year with my lack of professional academic writing skills. But because of this placement, I am really, really hopeful about my future and my grades for next year.

So yes. I cannot recommend a placement enough.

https://www.subscribepage.com/psychologyboxset

Thank you for reading.
I hoped you enjoyed it.
If you want a FREE book and keep up to date about new books and project. Then please sign up for my newsletter at
www.connorwhiteley.net/
Have a great day.

CHECK OUT THE PSYCHOLOGY WORLD PODCAST FOR MORE PSYCHOLOGY INFORMATION! AVAILABLE ON ALL MAJOR PODCAST APPS.

About the author:

Connor Whiteley is the author of over 60 books in the sci-fi fantasy, nonfiction psychology and books for writer's genre and he is a Human Branding Speaker and Consultant.

He is a passionate warhammer 40,000 reader, psychology student and author.

Who narrates his own audiobooks and he hosts The Psychology World Podcast.

All whilst studying Psychology at the University of Kent, England.

Also, he was a former Explorer Scout where he gave a speech to the Maltese President in August 2018 and he attended Prince Charles' 70th Birthday Party at Buckingham Palace in May 2018.

Plus, he is a self-confessed coffee lover!

A YEAR IN PSYCHOLOGY

<u>All books in 'An Introductory Series':</u>
Careers In Psychology
Psychology of Suicide
Dementia Psychology
Forensic Psychology of Terrorism And Hostage-Taking
Forensic Psychology of False Allegations
Year In Psychology
<u>BIOLOGICAL PSYCHOLOGY 3RD EDITION</u>
<u>COGNITIVE PSYCHOLOGY THIRD EDITION</u>
<u>SOCIAL PSYCHOLOGY- 3RD EDITION</u>
<u>ABNORMAL PSYCHOLOGY 3RD EDITION</u>
<u>PSYCHOLOGY OF RELATIONSHIPS- 3RD EDITION</u>
<u>DEVELOPMENTAL PSYCHOLOGY 3RD EDITION</u>
<u>HEALTH PSYCHOLOGY</u>
<u>RESEARCH IN PSYCHOLOGY</u>
<u>A GUIDE TO MENTAL HEALTH AND TREATMENT AROUND THE WORLD- A GLOBAL LOOK AT DEPRESSION</u>
<u>FORENSIC PSYCHOLOGY</u>
<u>THE FORENSIC PSYCHOLOGY OF THEFT, BURGLARY AND OTHER</u>

CRIMES AGAINST PROPERTY
CRIMINAL PROFILING: A FORENSIC PSYCHOLOGY GUIDE TO FBI PROFILING AND GEOGRAPHICAL AND STATISTICAL PROFILING.
CLINICAL PSYCHOLOGY
FORMULATION IN PSYCHOTHERAPY
PERSONALITY PSYCHOLOGY AND INDIVIDUAL DIFFERENCES
CLINICAL PSYCHOLOGY REFLECTIONS VOLUME 1
CLINICAL PSYCHOLOGY REFLECTIONS VOLUME 2
Clinical Psychology Reflections Volume 3
CULT PSYCHOLOGY
Police Psychology

A Psychology Student's Guide To University
How Does University Work?
A Student's Guide To University And Learning
University Mental Health and Mindset

OTHER SHORT STORIES BY CONNOR WHITELEY

<u>Mystery Short Stories:</u>
A Smokey Way To Go
A Spicy Way To GO
A Marketing Way To Go
A Missing Way To Go
A Showering Way To Go
Poison In The Candy Cane
Christmas Innocence
You Better Watch Out
Christmas Theft
Trouble In Christmas
Smell of The Lake
Problem In A Car
Theft, Past and Team
Embezzler In The Room
A Strange Way To Go
A Horrible Way To Go
Ann Awful Way To Go
An Old Way To Go
A Fishy Way To Go
A Pointy Way To Go
A High Way To Go
A Fiery Way To Go
A Glassy Way To Go
A Chocolatey Way To Go

Kendra Detective Mystery Collection Volume 1
Kendra Detective Mystery Collection Volume 2
Stealing A Chance At Freedom
Glassblowing and Death
Theft of Independence
Cookie Thief
Marble Thief
Book Thief
Art Thief
Mated At The Morgue
The Big Five Whoopee Moments
Stealing An Election
Mystery Short Story Collection Volume 1
Mystery Short Story Collection Volume 2

Science Fiction Short Stories:
Gummy Bear Detective
The Candy Detective
What Candies Fear
The Blurred Image
Shattered Legions
The First Rememberer
Life of A Rememberer
System of Wonder
Lifesaver

Remarkable Way She Died
The Interrogation of Annabella Stormic
Blade of The Emperor
Arbiter's Truth
Computation of Battle
Old One's Wrath
Puppets and Masters
Ship of Plague
Interrogation
Edge of Failure
One Way Choice
Acceptable Losses
Balance of Power
Good Idea At The Time
Escape Plan
Escape In The Hesitation
Inspiration In Need
Singing Warriors
Knowledge is Power
Killer of Polluters
Climate of Death
The Family Mailing Affair
Defining Criminality
The Martian Affair
A Cheating Affair
The Little Café Affair
Mountain of Death

Prisoner's Fight
Claws of Death
Bitter Air
Honey Hunt
Blade On A Train

<u>Fantasy Short Stories:</u>
City of Snow
City of Light
City of Vengeance
Dragons, Goats and Kingdom
Smog The Pathetic Dragon
Don't Go In The Shed
The Tomato Saver
The Remarkable Way She Died
The Bloodied Rose
Asmodia's Wrath
Heart of A Killer
Emissary of Blood
Dragon Coins
Dragon Tea
Dragon Rider
Sacrifice of the Soul
Heart of The Flesheater
Heart of The Regent
Heart of The Standing
Feline of The Lost

A YEAR IN PSYCHOLOGY

Heart of The Story
City of Fire
Awaiting Death

Other books by Connor Whiteley:

Bettie English Private Eye Series
A Very Private Woman
The Russian Case
A Very Urgent Matter
A Case Most Personal
Trains, Scots and Private Eyes
The Federation Protects

The Fireheart Fantasy Series
Heart of Fire
Heart of Lies
Heart of Prophecy
Heart of Bones
Heart of Fate

City of Assassins (Urban Fantasy)
City of Death
City of Marytrs
City of Pleasure
City of Power

Agents of The Emperor
Return of The Ancient Ones
Vigilance
Angels of Fire
Kingmaker

The Eight
The Lost Generation

Lord Of War Trilogy (Agents of The Emperor)
Not Scared Of The Dark
Madness
Burn It All Down

The Garro Series- Fantasy/Sci-fi
GARRO: GALAXY'S END
GARRO: RISE OF THE ORDER
GARRO: END TIMES
GARRO: SHORT STORIES
GARRO: COLLECTION
GARRO: HERESY
GARRO: FAITHLESS
GARRO: DESTROYER OF WORLDS
GARRO: COLLECTIONS BOOK 4-6
GARRO: MISTRESS OF BLOOD
GARRO: BEACON OF HOPE
GARRO: END OF DAYS

Winter Series- Fantasy Trilogy Books
WINTER'S COMING
WINTER'S HUNT
WINTER'S REVENGE

WINTER'S DISSENSION
<u>Miscellaneous:</u>
RETURN
FREEDOM
SALVATION
Reflection of Mount Flame
The Masked One
The Great Deer

<u>Gay Romance Novellas</u>
Breaking, Nursing, Repiaring A Broken Heart
Jacob And Daniel
Fallen For A Lie

www.ingramcontent.com/pod-product-compliance
Lightning Source LLC
LaVergne TN
LVHW011836060526
838200LV00053B/4057